248.4   Olson, Jake
OLS
             Open your eyes

DATE DUE			

PRAISE FOR *OPEN YOUR EYES*

"Jake Olson has been a source of tremendous inspiration for me since I met him, Emma, Brian, and Cindy, that fall day in 2009 in the middle of the Notre Dame field. Since then, and through the course of three features I've done with them and producer Nancy Devaney, I have learned how faith and love can enrich your life. Mine certainly has been because of the Olson family. And now, with *Open Your Eyes*, I can turn to any page on any given day and learn that lesson all over again. It is beautiful to read."

—SHELLEY SMITH, REPORTER, ESPN

"As I read the first chapter I was immediately drawn into Jake's writing, his spirit, and his passion. If you or anyone you know needs some hope or inspiration for their own lives, you need to buy this book. This story gave me hope as I read through the pages and I took a look at my own life in comparison to Jake's. Jake taught me so many valuable life lessons. This book will truly make you think and remind you that if you have the faith you can overcome anything."

—CHAD HYMAS, AUTHOR OF *DOING WHAT MUST BE DONE*, HALL OF FAME SPEAKER

"The story of Jake Olson and others not only uplifts the soul, but strengthens one's resolve to handle adversity with faith, vision, and a positive outlook. A very remarkable book about a very remarkable boy. I highly recommend it to everyone."

—HYRUM SMITH, COFOUNDER, FRANKLINCOVEY

This book is dedicated to Brian, Cindy, and Emma Olson. Thank you for your example, courage, and love.

OPEN
YOUR
EYES

OPEN YOUR EYES

10 UNCOMMON LESSONS TO DISCOVER A HAPPIER LIFE

JAKE OLSON
MCKAY CHRISTENSEN

NELSON
BOOKS

An Imprint of Thomas Nelson

Published in Nashville, Tennessee, by Nelson Books, an imprint of Thomas Nelson. Nelson Books and Thomas Nelson are registered trademarks of HarperCollins Christian Publishing, Inc.

Thomas Nelson, Inc., titles may be purchased in bulk for educational, business, fund-raising, or sales promotional use. For information, please e-mail SpecialMarkets@ThomasNelson.com.

Unless otherwise noted, Scripture quotations are taken from the King James Version.

Scripture quotations marked NIV are taken from the Holy Bible, New International Version®, NIV®. Copyright © 1973, 1978, 1984, 2011 by Biblica, Inc.™ Used by permission of Zondervan. All rights reserved worldwide. www.zondervan.com

ISBN 978-0-529-10269-0 (IE)

Library of Congress Cataloging-in-Publication Data

Olson, Jake, 1997-
 Open your eyes : 10 uncommon lessons to discover a happier life / Jake Olson, McKay Christensen.
    pages cm
 Includes bibliographical references.
 ISBN 978-1-4002-0581-3
 1. Happiness. 2. Success. I. Title.
 BF575.H27O47 2013
 248.4—dc23   2013021616

Printed in the United States of America

13 14 15 16 17 RRD 6 5 4 3 2 1

CONTENTS

FOREWORD

Suffering is not a prerequisite for happiness.

—JUDY TATELBAUM[1]

It didn't take long for Jake Olson to become one of us. In the fall of 2009, Jake's heart-wrenching story was brought to our attention at USC, just before he had the surgery that took away his vision. Jake was twelve years old and a huge Trojan fan, so we wanted to do anything we could to lift his spirits and give him some special memories. He and his family came to one of our midweek practices to get a behind-the-scenes look at our team, and many of our players immediately fell in love with him. They all joined together to chant his name when he came to the team meeting that day, something that will echo inside all of us forever. It also didn't take long for us to become so inspired by that extraordinarily precocious blond-haired kid from Orange County.

Just before his final surgery, Jake and his family joined us on the field for our road game at Notre Dame. We ended up pulling out a narrow victory that night in South Bend, Indiana, as Jake fired up the offensive line pregame and got to celebrate with us after the memorable win. He also came alongside us for a home game at the Coliseum shortly thereafter, and we were all woven together from then on. Jake's will to overcome his challenges had lit a fire inside all of us, and we were so grateful for the opportunity to have our paths align, a journey that continues to this day, even as Jake grows into a rising star in high school and as I've moved to coach in Seattle.

In football we talk a lot about competing, and Jake's living it out on a daily basis. He's fought to rise above circumstances that most others would run from or be crushed by. He's shown that nothing can hold him back—not countless surgeries, not blindness, not youth. Jake is the ultimate competitor, the pinnacle compliment in our football world and one that applies so precisely to him. Not only has Jake powered through his challenges, but he's become better for it and touched thousands of lives in the process. He's a natural leader, an eloquent speaker, a hilarious jokester, and a gifted athlete (have you seen his golf swing?!). And all this at age sixteen. Simply incredible and so inspirational.

Jake has pioneered what a triumphant life looks like. He's set an example for how to rise above challenges. He's overcome so much, and I have a feeling he's just getting warmed up. We're all excited to see where Jake goes from here—with all he's accomplished so far, no one should be surprised when he plays as the first blind golfer in the Masters. Keep fighting on, Jake. We're cheering as you continue to inspire us all.

Pete Carroll
Head Coach, Seattle Seahawks

INTRODUCTION

When I met Jake Olson in 2010, I was astounded at his uncommon faith. He has never known, until recent months, a life without cancer. Yet, instead of beating Jake down or leaving him helplessly dependent, cancer has made him strong and confident. He emerged from his battle with this merciless disease without his eyesight, but not blind. Not even close. He has used it as a springboard to soar into a rich and fulfilling life. Jake's story is inspiring, and within this story there are stirring lessons about how to open your eyes to a happy life.

Recently, I undertook a significant research study among North American adults to determine why only a small percentage of people can see their way through life with ease, and why many others seem blind or stuck, unable to progress. The research proved that our ability to see past our current circumstance and live by faith outweighed all other factors in determining happiness. Just like Jake Olson, those who were most mature and happy had confidence they'd persevere despite life's present challenges. The difference between happy and unhappy people comes down to a few simple things.

In this book, Jake and I will share these simple secrets to happiness. In the first chapters, you'll read Jake's story. In the chapters that follow, you'll read many other inspiring stories as Jake and I share simple concepts anyone can use to open their eyes to a happier way of life. In each chapter, as we talk about these concepts, Jake and his family give personal insights as to how they've applied them in their lives and family.

As we worked on this book, I was surprised at Jake's writing prowess. He's quick and thorough. He can articulate his thoughts clearly and concisely. He's written this book while getting top grades in school, playing football, taking golf lessons, learning to play the guitar, and facing life without physical sight for the first time. In short, his skill and effort are inspiring.

Jake and I met while making a presentation together. As we talked, I quickly realized that it wasn't Jake's battle with cancer that had given him his remarkable faith, but rather that his faith had given him a remarkable ability to live happily. His faith enables him to face cancer with a sense of humor, incredible ease, and a boost of enthusiasm. As we spent time talking, we discovered our common passion for helping others live by faith, and the idea for *Open Your Eyes* was born. In addition to writing books, Jake and I travel to speak to audiences around the country and host regular podcasts at openyoureyes.org to talk about principles of happiness.

We hope as you read this book you'll be uplifted and inspired to look at life and life's circumstances in a new, positive way. We also hope you'll find a few small things that, if done repeatedly, can bring about a new way of living. Most of all, we hope it brings you more joy and confidence that you *can* open your eyes to a happier life.

McKay Christensen

1

IT'S TIME TO SOAR

"For I know the plans I have for you," declares the LORD, "plans to prosper you and not to harm you, plans to give you hope and a future."

JEREMIAH 29:11 (NIV)

P*lease, no,* he thought. *Please, God, don't let it be like this.*
It wasn't black. He had expected black. He had expected the type of black you see when you close your eyes or when you're standing in a dark room with no light. But it wasn't like that.

After previous surgeries to remove cancer from his eyes, Jake had always kept his eyesight. He had been able to sense at least a glimmer of light leaking through the bandages. Not this time. This was brutally different. This lacked feeling altogether.

For the first time in his life, Jake was experiencing the complete loss of sight. Experts say our thinking, mood, and personality are inextricably linked to the visual stimuli we get from our eyes. If we're deprived of all visual sensation, depression sinks into our psyche.

For Jake, depression sets in when his friends talk about getting their driver's licenses, and he knows he will never have the experience of driving a car. It sets in when he wishes he could be on the football field experiencing the thrill of competition. Perhaps it is strongest when he's at school or hanging out with his friends, and because he can't see, he can't walk up to someone and engage in a conversation. He has to wait for them to say hello to him. Living in darkness can mean living in loneliness.

When the feeling of depression starts to sink in, like that day in the hospital, Jake has often thought to himself, *How could this be the plan God has for my life? What will my future be like? Why did this happen to me?* When Jake asks these questions, the answer is always the same: "'For I know the plans I have for you,' declares the LORD, 'plans to prosper you and not to harm you, plans to give you hope and a future.'"

God had a plan for Jake Olson the day he lost his eyesight. Without his sight, Jake's life would soar beyond all expectation. A miracle was about to happen. Can a blind boy open his eyes and see? Can God prosper you when you can't see a way out? For Jake Olson, the answer to those questions started on the football field . . .

Since it first fielded a team in 1888, the University of Southern California has been a dominating force in college football. In total, 472 USC Trojans have been taken in the NFL Draft, more than any other university.

In the 1920s, USC earned four national titles and became known as "the Thundering Herd." In the 1960s and 1970s, the Thundering Herd entered its golden age under the direction of coaches John McKay and John Robinson. Under McKay's leadership, the Trojans produced two Heisman Trophy winners, Mike Garrett and O. J. Simpson, and won four National Championships. Under Robinson, two more players won the Heisman: Charles White and Marcus Allen.

After the turn of the century, coach Pete Carroll and the quarterbacks took over the next golden age at USC. Carroll returned the Thundering Herd to national dominance. Quarterbacks Carson Palmer and Matt Leinhart both earned the Heisman. Under Carroll's leadership, USC won seven straight PAC-10 championships, and two National Championships in 2003 and 2004. In 2007, ESPN named USC the Team of the Decade.

A "Perfect Day" was a phrase coined by USC football announcer Peter Arbogast. It's a Saturday when USC wins, and USC's most notorious rivals, Notre Dame and UCLA, both lose. The last Perfect Day happened on September 11, 2010. That day USC beat Virginia, Notre Dame lost to Michigan, and UCLA lost to Stanford. In total, there have been twenty-six Perfect Days in USC history.

Perfect Day number twenty-five was October 17, 2009, and was perhaps the most perfect of all USC Perfect Days. On that day, USC beat Notre Dame at Notre Dame, and UCLA lost to California. What made it most memorable, however, was what happened off the field that day in South Bend, Indiana.

Waiting excitedly for the team bus to arrive at Notre Dame Stadium early that morning was twelve-year-old Jake Olson. Jake's father, Brian, is a USC graduate. Jake grew up in the decade of USC prominence. He knows the players by name and position. He is a walking encyclopedia of USC football information. He bleeds USC cardinal red and gold. Once USC football gets in your blood, you can't shake it. It sticks to you. It's all you talk about between August and January. Regardless of what's on the front page of the newspaper, you immediately flip to the sports page and read the latest news from the Trojan locker room.

As Jake waited anxiously with his family for the USC players to arrive at Notre Dame Stadium, his heart began to beat faster. He loves to see the bus rock back and forth as the players inside stand up and step off the bus. That day as players exited the bus, Jake greeted them with a high five and words of encouragement. On that Perfect Day, they had come to compete, and Jake was there to inspire them to victory.

Joining Jake and his family at Notre Dame were Shelley Smith and a crew of ESPN cameramen and producers. Smith, a reporter for ESPN *SportsCenter,* earned her first of four Sports Emmys in 1997 for her story on Magic Johnson and AIDS among athletes. That day she was working on another Emmy Award–winning story: Jake Olson and his final wish on this USC Perfect Day.

Smith had gotten word of Jake just a few days earlier. One of her crew had been on the USC practice field and told her about a boy visiting the team. She immediately reached out to USC's athletic department. "Our crew was at practice today and what I understand is this twelve-year-old boy has cancer in his eyes, or is blind, or is going to go blind. I'm not sure, but I guess he was at practice today. Can you tell me what is going on?"

What Shelley didn't know at the time was Jake had been diagnosed at eight months old with a rare form of eye cancer called *retinoblastoma*, leaving him with cancerous tumors in both eyes. His left eye was removed at ten months old, and he immediately began chemotherapy and cryotherapy to save his right eye. Miraculously, Jake's doctors were able to save it. This single eye had shown Jake his world for twelve years. Although the cancer had returned on eight different occasions, each time Jake was able to beat it.

In September 2009 the cancer returned once more. This time, however, the doctors ran out of miracles and options for viable treatment. The safest course of action, it was determined, was to remove Jake's remaining eye. The surgery was scheduled for November 2009, leaving Jake only a matter of weeks to take in all the sights of the world. As he contemplated his last few weeks of sight, Jake immediately thought of USC football. After surgery, he would never see a football game again.

Ever since he can remember, Saturdays have always meant one thing: USC football. Before he lost his eyesight for good, as one last wish, Jake wanted desperately to see a USC game up close. When news of Jake's wish reached head coach Pete Carroll, Carroll immediately invited Jake and his family to visit a USC practice session and team meeting.

When the family arrived at practice, they were enthusiastically greeted by Mark Jackson and others from the athletic department.

Within minutes they were being hugged and welcomed by Coach Carroll. Carroll insisted the entire Olson family, not just Jake, be invited into the pre-practice meetings that he directed with the assistant coaches. In front of all the players in the meeting room, the first thing Coach did was introduce Jake. As soon as the players heard about the boy, Coach Carroll's voice was drowned out with a roaring chant by all the players: "Jake, Jake, Jake, Jake . . ." It gave Jake and his family goose bumps.

They were then invited into the offensive line meeting led by Coach Pat Ruel. Jake's position on his little league football team was center, and his favorite player on the USC team was center Kris O'Dowd. Kris stands at six foot five and weighs three hundred pounds. He was the first true freshman in USC history to start a game at center. He was a first-team All American in high school and the anchor of the USC offensive line. Jake loved to watch Kris play.

Jake quickly bonded with Kris and the entire offensive line. As Coach Ruel roared through the Notre Dame game plan, Jake tossed out calls from the game book right on cue (with help from Kris). One of Jake's favorite moments came after a film session, when he got to say to offensive lineman Charles Brown, "Charles, hit that linebacker." The players laughed.

Coach Ruel, a thirty-four-year college and NFL coaching veteran, made Jake's wish of seeing USC players up close become a reality. With a kind heart and a twinkle in his eye, Coach Ruel made Jake a part of the USC offensive line. Jake felt right at home. After practice, the Olsons ate dinner with Kris and the other players in the athletic mess hall. There, nestled in the middle of a noisy squad of hungry athletes, sat Jake and his twin sister, Emma. They chatted with the players and Coach Carroll as if it were a family picnic. That day, a special relationship took root that would last a lifetime.

The Olsons received tickets to the USC–Notre Dame game from a friend, so they flew into South Bend the night before to watch the team go through their pregame walk-through.

When game day arrived, Jake was at the stadium early to welcome the team. As the players prepared for the game, Jake was on the field. Prior to kickoff, Jake fired up the offensive line. He was taking it all in and enjoying every minute of his new role! He would only have hours to enjoy these precious moments but a lifetime to remember them.

That day, something amazing happened in South Bend. It's what always happens when you get around Jake. He's inspiring. The coaches, players, and film crew were infused with extra faith and optimism because he was on the field.

Shelley Smith saw it right away. She could sense something special. She interviewed Coach Carroll with Jake at his side prior to kickoff, and the ESPN camera crew captured Jake's every move all day. Jake let them film, but he was too busy taking in the game to worry about what they were doing. It's what makes Trojan football so special for him; he has always been able to shift his attention from his pain to USC. Once again, facing the prospect of losing his sight in another painful surgery, Jake happily lost himself in USC football—only this time he was actually with the team!

The players were inspired by Jake's fearless spirit and went on to victory. Kris O'Dowd said, "How can a seventh grader make a hundred guys dead quiet and just hear every word that comes out of his mouth? It's because they have a mutual respect and love for this kid." O'Dowd later told Smith that he calls Jake his "little brother." He said, "Having Jake come into my life, really finding myself as a person and a man . . . I've learned a lot of lessons from him."

After the victory over the Irish, Jake was invited back to the locker room, where he shared in the celebration. Coach Carroll led the team in "Fight on for Victory." Jake got hugs from all the guys, including Matt Barkley, Joe McKnight, and of course, Kris O'Dowd.

Jake was inspiring others with his faith and determination long before ESPN found their way into his life. What ESPN did so incredibly well, however, was make it possible for millions to see and be inspired by Jake's life. His is one of the most recognized inspirational stories in the media today.

The ESPN video story captured the irreplaceability and precious-ness of Jake's final hours with physical sight. This was more than a wish come true; it was serious stuff. It was permanent memory-making for Jake. He was storing the last glimpses of football and friends in his mind. These sights would have to last an entire lifetime.

Jake was frantically memorizing how everything looked that day: the players, their faces, the way they moved, their long hair, their beards, and all the images of USC football. Coach Carroll made it possible. He was kind and generous. As Brian Olson, Jake's dad, said, "Coach Carroll is an amazing person. He had such compassion for Jake and our entire family and extended his hospitality to all of us. He especially included Emma in all the activities in which Jake was able to partici-pate. He innately knew that cancer affects everyone in a family, not just the person who has it. His warm welcomes and big hugs helped make this very difficult time easier for all of us. We'll be eternally grateful to Coach Carroll and the USC organization."

Jake would return to visit the USC football team a few weeks later, but this time without his sight . . .

Inseparably Connected

Jake and Emma are twins. This was part of God's incredible plan for their family. It's as if God knew what would happen to Jake and sent a twin angel to live with him. Jake and Emma share a special bond that has allowed his persevering spirit and her kind and protective nature to balance perfectly throughout their childhood. Emma was always by his side in school and always praying for him while he spent countless hours in the hospital.

With Emma by his side, Jake wasn't afraid. Her peace and optimism gave him the strength he needed to persevere. Emma would teach Jake the lessons he missed from school, help him keep up with his home-work assignments, and maintain his connections with friends and teachers. Because Emma made sure he stayed au courant with what was going on, Jake never missed a moment. Emma reported the details of everything Jake was missing. She helped him with homework and even organized messages from fellow students to lift Jake's spirits during the most difficult treatment sessions.

As time progressed and Jake's vision in his remaining eye deterio-rated, Emma became his "eyes," protecting him and leading him when necessary. Each of us has a God-given path, a calling to fulfill while we are here on earth. No doubt Emma was sent as Jake's twin to bless him. God knew he needed a guardian angel on earth.

But Emma also needed Jake. The lessons Emma has learned while sharing Jake's trials and treatments have shaped her character and given her tools she can use throughout her life. She understands how to cope with adversity almost as well as her brother. She knows how to trust in the Lord.

Emma's faith and confidence in God have been a blessing to the entire family. Through her prayers she has seen and experienced the tender mercies God bestows on his children. She has learned, through the whisperings of the Spirit, how to succor the weak and be an instru-ment in God's hands to bless those around her.

"Emma's faith that God would heal Jake and protect our family has never wavered," says Jake's mom, Cindy. "She is the solid rock of our family."

A Childhood with Cancer

Retinoblastoma is a malignant tumor of the retina that affects children under the age of six. It's rare: less than 3 percent of cancers in children are diagnosed as retinoblastoma. It occurs when a cell in the developing retina forms a mutation, causing it to grow out of control and become cancerous. In minor cases, it can be treated with laser surgery. In serious cases, such as Jake's, it threatens to spread to the brain and other parts of the body. Therefore, if radiation and other treatments fail, removal of the eye is the only treatment.

After doctors removed Jake's left eye at ten months old, Jake's parents did everything possible to help him keep his remaining eye. They traveled from their home in California to New York to participate in experimental treatments. One such treatment required a tube to be carefully threaded through Jake's main arterial system from his leg all the way to his eye to deliver chemotherapy. Each procedure lasted four to five hours with the risks of blindness and stroke. The family traveled to New York three times in an effort to kill the cancer. Before and after these procedures, Jake endured harsh radiation treatment. Jake knows the painful realities of fighting cancer.

INSIGHTS FROM JAKE

When I was six years old, my cancer returned. The tumor was large and it was leaking fluid. After six months of treatment, the doctors were recommending that my eye be enucleated, which would leave me blind. My parents didn't tell me about the doctor's recommendation.

During this challenging time of my life, God had put in my heart to get baptized. Although I was only six, I understood what this meant. I had been reading the Bible since the age of four and attending a Christian school, so I understood the Word and works of God. I made the decision during our Sunday service. God was pulling on my heart. I got baptized the next Sunday. The following Thursday, we went to what could have been my last checkup before the removal of my eye. But the cancer had disappeared. The doctors could not explain it because the treatments had not been working. It had seemed like the cancer was not receding. But during this exam, the cancer was gone. Completely gone. I knew God blessed me and rewarded my faith in him.

Turning to Their Faith

Upon learning of Jake's cancer at such an early age, the Olsons were devastated. The first thing they did was turn to the Lord. They had built their family on a foundation of faith, but that foundation would have to get stronger to endure what was ahead of them. Once they dealt with the devastating news, they decided to exercise their faith and move forward, taking each challenge one at a time. In their own words, "We serve the God of hope, and hope has never disappointed us."

As a toddler, Jake would set up an amphitheater in the living room and sit his family down. He would then inform everyone that he had a sermon prepared. He would give his sermon and lead the family in prayer. Jake's performances had a theatrical edge to them, but his faith was real. Jake has a tangible intimacy with the Lord, an intimacy that many believers never obtain. As Brian says, "Jake's level of faith and spirituality at age six made me step up as a Christian man to a higher level. Not just reading the Bible and praying, but how I lived and the actions I took. It made me grow in faith and action. Jake has a gift for inspiring others in a similar way."

When you ask Jake about his relationship with God, he gives such an authentic response that it leaves a lasting impression on you. Jake isn't shy about asking God to heal him; he has spent many hours asking for mercy. He believes in God's promises and knows good things

> "We serve the God of hope, and hope has never disappointed us."

come from God, not bad things, like disease. And God has answered Jake's prayers. While God has healed Jake's eyes of cancer many times, Jake recognizes that God has healed his soul, an order of magnitude far greater than simply removing cancer.

Jake's countless trips to the hospital transformed his outlook. At age eight, after one particular trip, he was heartbroken, even angered, by what he saw. As he walked the halls of the hospital, Jake saw numerous children around him battling cancer. From personal experience, he knew their pain and understood their discouragement. Jake decided to write a book as a source of comfort for them. He wanted to give them hope. Jake finished his book while continuing his own treatment that same year. His book of faith has been shared with thousands of kids, as well as adults, and has reached the far corners of the world on mission trips and outreach programs.

INSIGHTS FROM CINDY

When Jake decided to write his first book, he wanted to write about how Jesus helped him get through his fight with cancer. At the time, the cancer was in remission, and we thought Jake was completely healed. He wrote the book to give to other children who had cancer to offer them encouragement. When the book got printed, he took five hundred copies to the hospital so they could put it in their oncology department. The hospital refused to take it because it had a religious theme.

Jake was very disappointed and didn't know what to do. But God did. When we returned home there was a message on our machine from a local newspaper. They had heard about his book and wanted to do an interview with Jake. As soon as the interview was published, we started getting hundreds of calls from people asking how they could get a copy of the book. As the word spread, Jake's book was sent to many different countries. His book was placed in Ronald McDonald Houses, churches, and even our local library.

As Jake has learned over and over again, even if we face disappointment at first, if we stay in faith and trust in God, his plan will prove much bigger and better than we could ever imagine.

Jake's retinoblastoma is extreme. In total, he's had nine recurrences, endured twelve years of treatment, and battled discouragement the entire way. His spirits never dampened; he rarely let a situation get him down or strip him of hope. In almost every respect, Jake's life has remained relatively normal despite going through surgeries, chemotherapy and radiation treatments, medical procedures, and repeated trips to the doctor's office. He has taken everything in stride and kept pace with his schoolwork, friendships, and activities. God has protected him in so many ways. Jake's mom, Cindy, speaks of his faith, "Just to see his spirit grow, not shrink throughout these trials, is a testament to Jake's willingness to grow in his relationship with Christ." As Jake says, "God always has a plan. It may not be our plan, but it's the best plan."

> **If we stay in faith and trust in God, his plan will prove much bigger and better than we could ever imagine.**

Often, when the news came that the cancer had returned, Jake asked why. But it wasn't an angry *why*, just *why*. His belief that God would protect him and provide for him was always his first thought.

Talking about Jake's faith and his own, Brian said: "I would talk to him on the way home when he would call me from the car from one of his routine checkups and he would tell me the cancer was back, but that it would be all right. I can't explain it, but Jake's belief in God's promise was incredible. My fatherly instincts would kick in and say, 'This is wrong! Every part of it is wrong!' The visits to the hospital, the medication, the pain Jake would have to go through. Every time

I heard the news, it was wrong! The sadness, the gut-wrenching sickness of knowing Jake would have to go through more procedures, more pain, and more chemo. Each time I got the news, I couldn't eat, and I felt like throwing up. I would think, *Why, Lord? Why Jake?* Followed with, *Why can't I take this one for Jake? Please let me take this one.*"

As parents we have such a proclivity for love that it must come from heaven. Yet it is a small fraction of our *potential* to love, to love as God loves. It shows us how God wired us—with the capacity for real charity. But we don't let our full capacity out that often. If a disaster hits, we let it flow. If a child is hurt or sick, we let it flow. We are overcome with a deep-down feeling of love. Our hearts just ache. The love we have for our children is too rich to suppose it comes from any other source than from heavenly grace. It's the only possible explanation.

I've come to know that God loves us the same way. I can't put it any simpler than this: Jake feels the love of God. He feels it every day. Our God is not afraid to show us his love. He pursues us. He knocks on the door. For those of us willing to answer the knock, he will grace us with his presence.

God pursues each and every one of us. He reaches after us in the darkest hour.

Preparing to Live Without Sight

If you knew you only had a few days left to see the world with your eyes, what would you do? After his visit to the USC football games and practices, Jake turned to his other true love: golf. Jake loves to golf, and he's an exceptional player. So he started planning a golf trip up to Monterey Peninsula in Northern California. He wanted to play the famed Pebble Beach course before losing his sight.

Jake has been playing golf since the age of four and was developing his game nicely despite the loss of vision in one eye. Even with the harsh reality of losing his second eye, Jake remained unwilling to give up this dream. Golf would remain part of his life, whether he had sight or not. He still aims to become a professional golfer.

So Pebble Beach it was, and it turned out to be the last course Jake was able to play before losing his sight. Pebble Beach is carved into a truly distinct shoreline that captures the wonder of every golfer who is privileged with walking along its fairways. Once you've played Pebble Beach, it stays with you forever. Jake's foursome that day included his dad, one of his best friends, Evan, and Evan's dad.

"It wasn't this sad, dramatic round of golf," Brian said afterward. "It was a fun couple of days that included great golf, the kids jumping on the beds at the lodge, hitting balls into the ocean in the darkness of the night, and just goofing off. That round of golf, accentuated by the beauty of our surroundings, was just what Jake needed. He will remember the sights and experience forever."

If you ask Jake what he remembers about that day at Pebble Beach, he'll tell you that after the day of golf was done and they returned to their hotel room, he and Evan took all the pillows from the hotel room and threw them in the middle of the floor. Then they took turns climbing onto the couch and jumping off in dramatic fashion, slamming on top of the other in a reenactment of a professional wrestling "smackdown" session. They played, as twelve-year-old boys do, until they were worn to a frazzle.

With the days before the surgery quickly disappearing, Jake's anxiety began to grow. He would think, *Only five days left*, and the worry would return. The closer it came to the scheduled surgery date, the more distraught and afraid he became. He would later say that his anxiety was so high that he became more afraid of the day he'd lose his sight than of actually living sightless.

With only a few days left, Jake's final wish was to decorate the house for Christmas early so he could see the decorations one last time. Even though it was early November, the family woke up that

Saturday morning and crawled up into the attic to begin dropping down the twenty-five boxes of Christmas decorations. The Olsons love to decorate for Christmas! Jake's favorite decorations include the Charles Dickens Christmas Village, so they spent half the morning going through the usual ritual of setting it up. Jake's mom got the rest of the house gleaming with Christmas decorations and joy. Christmas songs played in the background. Cindy commented, "It was comforting that although the day to set up came earlier and perhaps under different circumstances, the entire day felt like a normal 'Let's get the house ready for Christmas' type day for us. That was such a comfort to me. It took our minds completely off the surgery. It just reminds us of how resilient and strong God created us when we allow his love to enter our hearts."

The Last Morning with Sight

The night before surgery, Jake attended USC football practice. Brian said, "Being at the practice and being with the guys, there wasn't this intensity of what we were confronting the next day. It turned out to be this sweet moment. I'll never forget it, and Jake won't either." Coach Carroll and the team encouraged Jake and invited him to come back as soon after the surgery as he could.

The day of the surgery arrived, and Jake's mom woke him in the early morning hours with a delicate kiss on his cheek. It was the type of kiss only a mom can give. The day had just started, but she couldn't stop crying. This started Jake crying, but he comforted his mother by saying, "Mom, don't worry. This is just going to be a new phase of my life."

> "Mom, don't worry. This is just going to be a new phase of my life."

As Jake rode in the car on the way to the hospital, he suddenly realized this was the last time he would see the outside world. He put his face against the window and desperately tried to take in all the sights his eyes and brain could record. He looked on one side of the car and then the other, trying to permanently place in his mind the images of the world around him. Out from under his glasses, tears were streaming down Jake's cheeks. It was more than his mom and dad could bear to watch.

As they checked into the hospital, and for most of the morning, they tried in vain to hold back the tears. A momentary blessing came when Kris O'Dowd arrived at the hospital. Jake's spirits picked up a bit, and Kris and Jake played a card game. But when the nurse came in to give Jake his IV, Jake started crying, Brian and Cindy started crying, and Kris, this mountain of a man, started crying. Kris went over to Jake, gave him a kiss on the head, and said, "You're the strongest kid I've ever known. Keep being who you are and everything will work out." Jake said the hardest part of the entire experience was right then, knowing those were his last minutes of sight.

INSIGHTS FROM CINDY

Since Jake was a baby, he has always sat on my lap while waiting at the hospital. No matter how old he got, he would sit on my lap. No matter how tall he got or how much he weighed, as soon as I sat down to wait with him, he would crawl onto my lap.

On the morning of the surgery that would take his sight and remaining eye, as we were waiting for surgery, Jake came over and sat on my lap. He was twelve years old and taller than me. He covered my body. I knew this was where he felt safe and comforted, and I put my arms around him and held him tight. I would have gladly traded places with him if I could have. I would have taken away the pain if I could have.

When things get to be too stressful and overwhelming, I crawl onto Jesus' lap. It is the place I feel safe and comforted, and he wraps his loving arms around me and holds me tight.

It's Time to Soar

After the surgery, the first thing Jake heard was the sound of his mom's voice. He said, "I really didn't feel sorrow because it's already happened; I can move on and do whatever I want. I don't have to worry about it anymore. I don't have to worry about that day coming. It's already happened."

Six days after his surgery, Jake returned to the USC team meeting and was greeted by Coach Carroll and his friends on the team. Jake told them, "The day has come and gone and you can't do anything about that day anymore. All you can do is move on." And Jake has done that.

Not only has Jake moved on, but his life is soaring. Jake is more determined than ever to golf on the PGA Tour. He has a golf coach. He golfs on his high school team. He is taking his skill and his will to compete to a whole new level. Jake has learned to play the guitar and has remained an honor roll student. He has served on student council. Jake played football with his team right up to his surgery date, and amazingly, played a play-off game without sight five days after his surgery.

> "When things get to be too stressful and overwhelming, I crawl onto Jesus' lap. It is the place I feel safe and comforted, and he wraps his loving arms around me and holds me tight."

Jake has continued to play with his team, starting at center. He has a knack for making perfect snaps and knows how to block. His sharpened sense of hearing serves him well. He can't see 'em, but he can hear 'em! During the season, his coach drew up a couple of plays for Jake at the quarterback position. One was a running play, and the second a passing play. Jake ran for five yards and a first down, and then completed a touchdown pass to a teammate in the end zone. Yes, Jake threw a touchdown pass!

Jake and his dad play catch with the football in a very unique way. When Brian claps his hands, Jake knows in which direction to throw the ball. Jake has a great sense of direction, and he usually hits Brian right in the chest. So Jake didn't have much trouble when it came to throwing a touchdown pass in a real game.

Since her original ESPN video story aired, Shelley Smith has continued to report on Jake's progress. She wrote a story about Jake's touchdown triumph. As part of her report, Jake told her, "I knew where my wide receiver was going to be, and he was lined up to my left. I knew that he was going to be doing a post over the field and he was going to clap his hands. . . . I really didn't hear his clap, but I kind of waited and threw it in the middle of the field, and it was perfect." Jake's mother, Cindy, said it was like a scene out of a movie. "The coach on the other team cried," she said. "And then everyone was crying."

Jake appeared as a guest analyst on ESPN's *College GameDay*. It was New Year's Day, and Jake had to wake up at 4:00 a.m. He had prepared by studying the current college rankings, team statistics, and writing his predictions for the college bowl game scores. Once on the air, he and Coach Lee Corso quickly began to disagree on the final picks. Jake had the final word, however, picking the winners 6–4 and predicting more accurately than Coach Corso!

With all this going on, Jake and Emma still find time to hit the road and help others. They visited Costa Rica in the summer of 2010 on a mission trip with other classmates from their school. Jake has also traveled to the four corners of the United States to deliver motivational speeches. It's safe to say Jake has inspired tens of thousands of people at sporting events, youth rallies, fund-raisers, and business conventions. He made a guest appearance at Dick Vitale's V Foundation event, which raised more than one million dollars to fight pediatric cancer.

Jake visited Coach Carroll, who's now with the Seattle Seahawks, to motivate high school seniors as part of the Seahawks' outreach program. Jake and Kris O'Dowd stay in touch. Jake attended Kris's college graduation celebration. They remain close friends.

Jake visits middle and high schools to encourage students who might be struggling, and to deliver his message of perseverance and faith. Jake recently spoke to a large group of blind students. Facing a life without vision can be immensely disheartening. Jake spoke to them about faith and about realizing your potential, whatever that might be.

Recently Jake was a guest on *Katie* (the Katie Couric show). Jake tells audiences like Couric's that he may have lost his sight, but not his vision. Jake will never be without vision. Jake sees things that we can't even comprehend. He sees light and hope in a situation that others might find hopeless. He has more optimism for his

> Despite his circumstances, Jake never ends up more than a few inches away from the Lord.

future than one could imagine. Despite his circumstances, Jake never ends up more than a few inches away from the Lord.

Inspiring Others

In late August 2010, Jake and his family were in Hawaii for the University of Southern California's football season opener. Jake and

Emma had spent the previous eight months waiting for the season to begin, and it finally arrived! The trip to Hawaii for the opener was a perfect way to start the season.

The day following an exciting USC win over the University of Hawaii, the Olsons were enjoying dinner at a restaurant nestled along the North Shore when a gentle Hawaiian man approached their table insistent on introducing himself. He was anxious to share something important with the Olsons, and with Jake in particular.

He told Jake he counsels and is a parent to foster children. One of his foster kids, a seventeen-year-old young man, had seen the ESPN video featuring Jake during the college football broadcast the prior year on Thanksgiving weekend. The young man came from a family of drug addicts, was having trouble in school, and at the time, couldn't seem to move forward in a productive way. He was clearly at a crossroads in his young life. When the young man saw Jake's story on ESPN, he decided at that moment that he was going to change his life. If Jake Olson could courageously face cancer, lose his sight, and continue facing life with optimism and hope, then he could at least graduate from high school and go to college. Then the Hawaiian man smiled and said, "My foster son kept his promise. In June he finished high school, and started his first day of college last week."

What many people don't know is that there is much more to Jake and his family than can be viewed in a nine-minute ESPN video. If you look closely at Jake's life, it proves to be bountifully rich with inspirational lessons. His faith, perseverance, and approach to life are his real story.

2

UNCOMMON FAITH

The man who insists on seeing with perfect
clearness before he decides, never decides.

—HENRI FREDERIC AMIEL

On August 9, 2010, on the shores of Lake Michigan, 156 of the world's elite golfers assembled to battle the rugged windswept terrain of Whistling Straits at the 2010 PGA Championship. Nestled in Kohler, Wisconsin, "the Straits," as they are called, offer up fierce obstacles that intimidate the average golfer. But the huge sandy areas, deep pot bunkers, and undulating greens didn't seem to faze the field of professionals that arrived to compete in the PGA's perennial event.

In true competitive form, the pros from twenty-three different countries went about their practice rounds and tournament preparation in businesslike fashion, each one competing for millions of dollars in prize money with $1.35 million going to the winner. Included in the 2010 lineup were Ernie Els of South Africa and Vijay Singh of Fiji. In 2004, Singh had prevailed in the championship at the Straits in a three-way play-off against Justin Leonard and Chris DiMarco. It was an amazing turnaround for the then forty-one-year-old Fijian who, despite closing with a 76, was perfect in the three-hole play-off to win. Also competing in the 2010 field were Americans Phil Mickelson, Jim Furyk, and superstar Tiger Woods, who was clinging to his number one ranking.

Something unexpected happened, however, as the players began their first round on Thursday. Dense fog settled in on the rolling fairways of the Straits. Players couldn't see the flag even on the short par 3 holes. They were hitting into a blinding mass of grey. That day, seventy-eight golfers were unable to finish their round.

Fog can wreak havoc on a major golf tournament. Players who sneak in their round before the fog arrives or after it clears can end up several strokes ahead of those stuck in the grey, settling cloud. The second day was no better. The fog took its toll again, delaying start times and leaving others stranded on the course, unable to finish. The result? Almost all the big names in golf never recovered, including Mickelson, Woods, and Singh. The German Martin Kaymer, a lesser-known player at the time, walked away with the championship.

How could the best golfers in the world be handicapped so severely by fog? Golf is a game dominated by those who have two important skills: exceptional muscle memory and outstanding vision. Why vision? Unlike the pros, when the average golfer steps up to the tee, he sees the sand trap to the left, the water hazard ahead, and the trees to the right. He thinks about these hazards and says to himself something like, "Don't hit it in the trees." This prevailing thought affects his swing, creating the slight uncertainty that tilts the club face or slows his rotation. When pros step up to the tee, they focus exclusively on the exact landing place for their shot on the green or the fairway. They visualize the proper distance and direction. They don't see the hazards, only where they want to end up. Vision is essential to a swing of certainty.

But in foggy conditions, even the pros can't see the landing place or picture where they want the ball to arrive. Their sight is inseparably connected to their swing. They may have caddies who can perfectly describe the slope or width of the greens from memory, GPS readings of the distance to the hole, or they might have even traversed the course themselves hundreds of times. Despite all these obvious advantages, they can't prevail without clear vision.

Life is very much the same. We may be the very best at what we do. We may handle life's challenges well enough in clear weather. But when fog starts creeping into our thoughts, when we begin to let doubt and fear take root, we get intimidated and stop moving. When things are unclear, unknown, or unsure, we freeze. Without vision, we can't act with certainty or courage.

Perhaps you're battling an unexpected illness, struggling in a marriage, or facing financial difficulties. When we give in to these foggy conditions, we get discouraged, and things can seem much worse than they really are. We're blind to where we are going. Faith, however, can lift that fog of discouragement and empower us to rise above the dense vapor that has settled over our perspective.

When things are foggy and we can't see how they will improve, with uncommon faith we can, like Jake Olson, press forward as if there is no fog at all! God uses life's hazards to see if we'll have faith in him, and when we do, he blesses us with the ability to walk in the midst of those challenges with strength and courage. It's interesting that those with uncommon faith can clearly imagine their

> Those with uncommon faith can clearly imagine their future despite their current situation. They're focused on their landing place, not the hazards.

futures despite their current situations. They're focused on their landing place, not the hazards. Even in the fog of uncertainty, they swing
with accuracy and speed.

Jake Olson swings away at life every day. He says his goal is to be
the first blind golfer on the PGA Tour. Imagine if Jake would have
been one of the 156 pros at Whistling Straits. The fog would have had
no impact on his game whatsoever! He could golf in the fog as well as
in the sunshine. In fact, it would have been just like any other day on
the course for Jake. In my mind's eye I can see Jake as a pro, finishing
his round at Whistling Straits while Tiger Woods and Phil Mickelson
return to the clubhouse!

INSIGHTS FROM JAKE

It's true! Fog wouldn't impact my game at all. But let's get one thing clear;
there's one thing visually impaired golfers don't like: cactus! Especially the
ones with white, puffy ends, *jumping cholla* cactus, more affectionately
called "teddy bears." They literally jump at you and stick in your skin. It's
probably one of the main reasons I have learned to drive the ball straight
off the tee.

Someone once told me that you can't hit a good putt; all you can
do is make a good stroke. Being without sight lets me be completely
focused on executing a good golf swing without being distracted.
Whether it's Phil, Tiger, or me, the only thing we can do is execute our
swing and leave the other things out there, the things that we can't control, to God.

It's a great metaphor for my life right now. There are lots of things
I can't control anymore. But what's opened up for me is the ability to
focus better than I ever could before on what's right in front of me. That
makes things easier in a way. Then I can trust in God for the rest.

Nowadays, when I'm golfing I focus almost exclusively on my

swing. I used to focus on all the elements out of my control, like the rough or the hazards. Now I can't see them. It seems to me, when we face obstacles, if we only focus on what we can control, things become a little easier.

My battle with cancer is very similar. Successfully fighting cancer is about not letting outside variables, the things you can't control, dominate your thoughts. I put my focus on God's promises, his presence, and his comfort. This focus is something I have control over; all the other elements are out of my control. It's a simple concept, yet it's also very powerful. I focus on the things I can impact and leave the fog, rain, and darkness in life to God.

> "I focus on the things I can impact and leave the fog, rain, and darkness in life to God."

Believe it or not, when I swing the golf club, I still visualize. When I swing, I actually have to keep my eyes open. My brain knows if my eyes are open or shut. If I keep them shut, I can't even hit the ball. I rely on a mental visualization of the ball and my swing. My golf swing requires my eyes to be in communication with my brain. But I am also relying on my other senses, like feeling the weight of the club, feeling for my balance, feeling for my tempo, and feeling if the club head is open or closed.

Don't get me wrong. Do I wish I had my eyes to see the beauty of Pebble Beach when I play it again? Absolutely! Eyes can serve one well, but at the same time they can prove to be a handicap. As an example, eyes can deceive you on the putting green. It's been proven that only one out of four golfers can rely upon their eyes to properly read the curves and slopes in a green. The other three out of four have flaws in their sight that make them see things that really aren't there. No joke. I'm learning to use my feet to sense the slope of the green. I have become quite skillful at reading the breaks in a green just by pacing my line of putt.

Jack Nicklaus, winner of eighteen major PGA championships, said:

I never hit a shot, not even in practice, without having a very sharp, in-focus picture of it in my head. First I see the ball where I want it to finish, nice and white and sitting up high on the bright green grass. Then the scene quickly changes, and I see the ball going there—its path, trajectory, and shape, even its behavior on landing. Then there is a sort of fade-out, and the next scene shows me making the kind of swing that will turn the previous images into reality.[1]

Jake Olson may not have his physical sight, but he can still visualize his golf shot, imagine the scene, and connect that image to the type of swing that will turn his shot into reality. And while Jake has the huge disadvantage of not having physical sight to see the course, he has the hidden blessing of not being able to see the hazards. He knows they're there, but he can swing without letting them cloud his vision.

The same works for us. When we claim faith, we choose not to worry about or even see the hazards. We choose to focus on the landing place for our life. As a result, we lose our worry and anxiety over the things that stand in our way, freeing up energy and focus that can carry us beyond our fears and challenges. Jake takes a similar approach to life. He sees where he wants to go and doesn't worry about the "small" obstacles—like being blind.

In the weeks leading up to Jake's surgery, as any parent would, Jake's parents cried and worried. *What will Jake be able to do without his sight? How will he function normally in his teenage years? How will he adjust? What does the future hold for him?* Any parent can imagine the feelings of sadness and disquiet at having a twelve-year-old son lose his sight permanently. But as Brian said, "Jake just took it in stride and didn't give it a second thought. It was just matter of fact: 'Okay, I am blind. I can deal with it. What's next?' He's been a great example to us. He does more than hold on to his faith: he lives his faith."

Some Miracles Just Take Time

When I met Jake, I was reminded of my first meeting with Art Berg fifteen years ago. I see the same uncommon faith in Jake today that I saw in Art then.

On December 26, 1983, at the age of twenty-one, Art Berg was soon to be married. He was traveling late at night. His friend John was driving and fell asleep. As the car veered off the road, both Art and John awoke. John tried desperately to avoid a cement barrier but couldn't. The Volkswagen struck the barrier and rolled several times down the side of the freeway. Despite wearing a safety belt, Art was thrown from the car as it rolled over and over. When Art regained consciousness, he was lying helplessly on the dust of the Nevada desert, and he couldn't feel his legs. Art had broken his neck. He was left a quadriplegic.

Art's doctor told him that he had lost the use of his feet and his legs, his stomach muscles, two of his three chest muscles, and most of his shoulder and arm muscles. He told Art that he would need help for the rest of his life to eat, get dressed, and to move from place to place. He also told Art that he would likely never drive, work, have children, or play any kind of sports.

I met Art twelve years after his accident. By that time, Art had married his fiancée, Dallas, and they were the parents of two children. Art had set a world record as a quadriplegic by completing an ultra-wheelchair marathon of more than 325 miles from Salt Lake City to St. George, Utah, in record-setting time. He was a best-selling author, successful business owner, and accomplished motivational speaker.

Art had an amazing spirit of uncommon faith. He wrote, "That same Master who calmed the tempest of the sea also calms my storms and yours. While not always removing the storms from our lives, he replaces fear with faith, and doubt with understanding."[2]

Art traveled more than two hundred thousand miles a year as a motivational speaker. He often traveled alone, self-sufficient. He could feed himself and drive a car. When we would pick up Art at the airport, he would usually have someone from the flight still talking to him. People loved being around him. His courage was uplifting and contagious. He said:

> Struggle and pain ... were not put here to torment or mock men, but to lift and build them. .... Adversity, pain, and struggle do not challenge the Lord's love for us, they prove it. To those who love God, the stony, rough way becomes a blessing and an opportunity for miracle after miracle. The rewards are sweeter and the panorama before them more beautiful than the way of ease and instantaneous miracles. When we are denied immediate relief from our heartache, tears, or tragedy, it is because there is a better way that will teach us more and work for our ultimate good. Some miracles just take time. Thank God for that![3]

Art was awarded the Consummate Professional Speaker of the Year in 1998 and the International Lions' Humanitarian of the Year Award in Washington, DC, in 1999. He died in 2002, at the age of thirty-nine, from an adverse reaction to medication. Art left a legacy of uncommon faith by the way he lived his life and faced adversity. It's not what happens to us; it's what we do with what happens to us that matters!

INSIGHTS FROM JAKE

People often ask, "Why does God put struggles in my life?" The truth is that he only allows things to happen and isn't the cause of them. But it's through our perseverance in these situations that we build our character and bring glory to him. The only tricky thing is that we have to be patient. I had to stay patient for twelve years until I knew what God was doing in my life. God has his own time and plan to prosper you; not to harm you, but to give you hope and a future.

I put my faith in his promises. One of his promises is that in all things he works for the good of those who love him. God's promise is for *all* things, not *some* things. Losing my sight is included in *all* things. I trust that somehow and some way I will be used for his glory.

I put complete trust in Jeremiah 29:11: "'For I know the plans I have for you,' declares the Lord, 'plans to prosper you and not to harm you, plans to give you hope and a future'" (NIV). It gives me encouragement and hope. This verse has helped me get through some of the most difficult times and challenges.

God can turn a bad situation into a good one. Always trust the Lord and put your faith in him. "Faith is the substance of things hoped for, the evidence of things not seen" (Heb. 11:1).

> "Faith is the substance of things hoped for, the evidence of things not seen" (Heb. 11:1).

Hope is my foundation and it helped me get through a lot of dark days. Faith doesn't take away fear or remove a challenge, but faith helps you get through it. I would be lying if I said my fight didn't include moments of fear. I heard a definition of courage once, and I really liked it: "Courage is being fearful but doing it anyway." My courage, my strength, and my perseverance all start with my faith.

By Small and Simple Things Are Great Things Brought to Pass

C. S. Lewis wrote:

Every time you make a choice you are turning the central part of you, the part of you that chooses, into something a little different from what it was before. And taking your life as a whole, with all your innumerable choices, all your life long you are slowly turning this central thing either into a heavenly creature or into a hellish creature.[4]

I knew a truly Christian man who was battling an advanced form of terminal cancer. During his chemotherapy sessions he was terribly sick. He was depressed. One day he thought to himself, *I wish I could die right now.* He picked up his Bible and read the words Jesus spoke of forgetting ourselves and giving to those around us. He thought to himself, *I can't even get out of bed. What can I do for others in this pitiful condition?* Then inspiration came: *You can call those in need and write letters of encouragement to those who are suffering.* So he started. He made one phone call or wrote one letter a day. His words of encouragement lifted others, and his newfound purpose lifted him.

Uncommon faith will work when all else has stopped working. We can embrace the things we cannot see. We can take action. We can rely on the strength of others. We can place our faith in God. We can do small and simple things to bring about our end goal. We can take a lesson from Jake Olson and live with uncommon faith.

My first meeting with Jake was impressive. But equally impressive are Jake's parents. They're kind, patient, and faithful. Their courage in facing Jake's lifelong battle with cancer has been demonstrated by small acts of faith.

INSIGHTS FROM BRIAN AND CINDY

As parents, we can think of nothing as precious as a newborn baby—except two newborns within minutes of each other. We had prayed for many years that God would bless us with a child, and now we were doubly blessed. We quickly adapted to our new routine of feeding, changing diapers, burping, and then feeding again. There is not much sleep to be had with twins.

Emma, Jake's twin sister, weighed a tiny five pounds, four ounces and was colicky. So, when we brought her and Jake home from the hospital, she literally cried for the first seventy-two hours. She didn't eat or sleep; she just cried. We were helpless and we didn't know what to do. Nothing can prepare you for the likes of your newborn baby girl crying with no relief in sight. It was the first of many moments that made us realize what little we knew about parenting and at the same time what an inexplicable affinity we had for it.

Since the moment the doctors told us our infant son had malignant cancer in both eyes and that his left eye needed to be removed to save his life, we have felt the power of God's love. When we heard that at age five his cancer had returned, we felt it again. When we heard that, at age twelve, after battling cancer for seven more years, he was going to lose his right eye and would be blind, God's love got us through. Every moment of every surgery required God's love. Every shot, every treatment, the delivery of every chemo drug required God's love. God's love also reached Jake. It was Jake's acceptance of God's love that gave him strength to endure and battle cancer so courageously.

When Jake was six years old, he was scheduled to have another early-morning surgery. About 5:30 a.m. we were waiting in the pre-op room before Jake was taken in. In the pre-op room was a young mother waiting with her child, who was also headed to surgery. Jake got up, went over, sat down next to the mother, and asked her why her child was there.

She told Jake about her child's illness and surgery that would happen that day. Jake, with no hesitancy, asked her if she believed in Jesus and if she prayed. Jake told her about his cancer and explained how Jesus helped him to not be afraid. He told her to tell her child about prayer and Jesus, so he wouldn't be afraid either. As Jake left to play with the toys in the waiting area, this young mother turned to me with tears in her eyes. She told me she had lost her faith a long time ago, but that after listening to Jake, she was going to start praying again.

Jake has been put under anesthesia more than fifty times during his young life. Every time, just before they would wheel him into the surgical ward, he would tell me he visualized Jesus lying right next to him in the bed. He knew Jesus was with him and protecting him.

We have often wondered, *Why our family? Why did this happen to us?* One simple answer is that we've learned to rely on our faith. We are brought to our knees almost every day, and there we have learned to accept what God has to offer. We were a faithful family before, but Jake's cancer has made us a family full of faith. God chose us to be Jake's and Emma's parents. We know that for certain. Not a day goes by that we don't pray for them. And the grace of God has never failed us. It is something for which we will be eternally grateful.

The days and hours leading up to Jake's surgery to remove his only remaining eye were fraught with a spectrum of emotions. Jake had his, Emma had hers, and we had ours. Words were difficult. Yet there was no shortage of love. It just kept flowing, endless love and hope and strength. We prayed together, held hands, laughed together, and cried together. As the days grew nearer to the surgery, the fog grew thicker. Life grew harder. Yet our prayers grew deeper. In our weakest moments, God's strength was perfected. God's words were vibrant, his presence evident. God placed in our hearts the conviction that Jake's life without sight would be a brand-new phase for him and that he would soar!

As all parents know, the love we have for our children is a unique sort of love. We've been blessed with a glimpse into the love our heavenly Father has for each and every one of us. We've put our faith in that love. It got us through our darkest moments. We know our heavenly Father loves us and will reach out for us in our time of need, as many times as we need.

God Will Bless the Mighty in Faith

In Mark 10:46–52 we read a story of uncommon faith—the story of blind Bartimaeus, who sat by the highway, begging. It's believed that beggars in Jericho at the time wore a garment bearing a special insignia that certified their pitiful condition to be genuine and gave them "license" to beg. Bartimaeus wore such a garment. When he heard it was Jesus of Nazareth who was walking nearby, he cried out saying, "Jesus, thou Son of David, have mercy on me." To call Jesus the "Son of David" was to call him the prophesied Messiah. To say this publicly was dangerous, to say the least. Men could be punished or killed for making such a declaration in public.

When he was told to be quiet, Bartimaeus cried even louder again, "Jesus, thou Son of David, have mercy on me." After his undaunted demonstration of faith, Jesus called to the blind man. The Scripture says, "And he, casting away his garment, rose, and came to Jesus." Bartimaeus threw off his garment knowing that he would never be a beggar again. Based on this demonstration of faith, the Lord gave Bartimaeus his sight, telling him his faith had made him whole.

When we choose faith, even in small ways, we free ourselves to discard our prior reputation or habits. We can leave them behind and start a new way of thinking. We can cast away our garment of fear or discouragement and act with confidence that our life is going to soar. We can say, "I know that the doctors have said I have cancer, but it will not control the rest of my life. I will live in faith." Or "I know I am now divorced. But it will not define me. I know there is a wonderful person waiting for me. I will have new and fulfilling relationships in my future."

When he lost his sight, Jake refused to wear the insignia of "handicapped" or "helpless." He chose not to be defined by his new obstacle. Jake's choice was to throw off the coat of fear and define his life in different ways. He opened up the door for opportunity and mighty blessings.

When you ask Jake about his life, he first and foremost humbly and appropriately declares his faith in the Lord. By doing so, he genuinely hopes others will take Jesus Christ as their source of strength. Jake has never worn the garment of the beggar, like most people would expect him to, but declares his faith to anyone who asks. His faith and testimony give him peace and strength, and he wants others to have the same peace in their lives. He has shrugged off the coat of self-pity and taken a step of faith toward Jesus.

INSIGHTS FROM JAKE

As a kid I did not like shots. I didn't throw a fit or cry, but the shots were painful. Sometimes the shots were IVs or white blood count shots due to chemotherapy. So, I developed a way to help endure the pain. I would hold out my other hand as if I was grasping thin air but I pretended I was grabbing Jesus' hand. I started doing this at a young age and I still do it today and it eases my pain. I cannot explain why the pain was lessened, but it was.

For those who are going through hard times, my advice is this: Life is a gift from God and not a possession of man. Every day is a miracle waiting to happen. God has a plan for us and loves us. We need to recognize how much we are loved by God and that we have a purpose here on earth. Life is given to us for a reason. We need to find that reason and glorify God in doing so.

Life is a gift. If you waste that gift being stressed-out about friends or school, then you are also wasting God's plan for you. God put you here on earth to glorify him. We can glorify him in schoolwork, as well as playing sports, as well as setting an example to our peers in public. Every minute of every day we can point our actions to God.

When we face trials in life with faith, we can transcend habits and behavior that would otherwise keep us from being happy. In John 9:6–7 Jesus saw a man who had been blind from his birth. Jesus "spat on the ground, and made clay of the spittle, and he anointed the eyes of the blind man." Then he told the man to go wash in the pool. The man was healed.

This scripture is full of imagery for us. When we have faith in the words that have come out of the Lord's mouth and mix them with this earthly experience (just as Jesus mixed spittle with the dust of the earth), we can make the miraculous happen, overcome adversity, and grow into the people the Lord intended for us to become. Once again, C. S. Lewis:

> Imagine yourself a living house. God comes in to rebuild that house. At first, perhaps, you can understand what He is doing. He is getting the drains right and stopping the leaks in the roof and so on: you knew those jobs needed doing and so you are not surprised. But presently he starts knocking the house about in a way that hurts abominably and does not seem to make sense. What on earth is He up to? The explanation is that He is building quite a different house from the one you thought of—throwing out a new wing here, putting on an extra floor there, running up towers, making courtyards. You thought you were going to be made into a decent little cottage: but He is building a palace.[5]

In Summary

- It's not what happens to us; it's what we do with what happens to us that matters.
- Press forward with faith *no matter what*!
- By small and simple things are great things brought to pass.
- God will bless the mighty in faith.

3

OPEN YOUR EYES

Where there is no vision, the people perish.

—PROVERBS 29:18

At first he wasn't worried—he'd had minor problems with vision shifts in the past—but on this day, high-altitude climber Beck Weathers couldn't even see his own feet! What made his temporary vision loss potentially deadly was the fact he was climbing in the predawn darkness at 27,500 feet on his final push to the top of Mount Everest.

His hope was that with the rising of the sun his vision would return. Eye surgery eighteen months earlier had altered his corneas, and the high altitude had rendered him blind. So Weathers stepped aside to let other climbers pass in hopes that his vision would improve and he could continue.

Weathers, a pathologist from Dallas, had spent most of his adult years obsessed with climbing. He'd put climbing ahead of his family, time with his children, and other priorities in life. In his early thirties, as he battled depression, he fed his dark obsessions by losing himself in one extreme climb after another. His wife, Peach, had objected to his trip to Everest. But her wishes had gone unheeded as he disappeared for months to pursue his fixation on climbing the highest peak in the world.

Beck arrived on Everest in the 1996 climbing season eager to scale the ultimate mountain. Everything was in place for a successful summit. He had signed up with professional guide Rob Hall and Hall's company, Adventure Consultants. They had spent weeks acclimatizing for their final ascent to the top of the tallest mountain in the world.

The team of climbers joining Beck included author Jon Krakauer, Japanese climber Yasuko Namba, guide Andy Harris, and six others. They started their final summit bid in earnest on May 9 after negotiating the Khumbu Icefall and the four-thousand-foot Lhotse Face. For the final two days, the climbers would use bottled oxygen full-time. At these altitudes, your body deteriorates in a matter of hours without oxygen. On May 10, the plan was to leave advanced camp in the early morning hours, thereby allowing for a summit attempt around noon, giving them time to return safely to the tents at high camp before nightfall.

Beck was feeling strong in the early morning hours as he fell in line with his teammates. But after his vision faded, he told Rob Hall that he would wait for a few hours and follow the others to the top if his vision returned. Rob agreed as long as Beck promised he would wait for Hall if anything went wrong, so they could descend to the tents safely together. Beck agreed, not knowing that his promise would nearly seal his fate.

Hall's team and the other climbers ascending that day were delayed by one mishap after another, and most arrived atop Everest hours after the predetermined turnaround time of early afternoon. Farther down the mountain, Beck's vision never returned, and as climber after climber returned from the top, they passed Beck, asking him to join them in their descent to the safety of the tents. But Beck stayed true to his promise to Hall and waited patiently in the cold.

Beck waited until late afternoon, by which time he was sinking fast. His oxygen was gone. The effects of hours at high elevation where the oxygen is deathly thin left him shivering, weak, and sinking into apathy. What Beck didn't know was that Hall was still on top of Everest with serious problems of his own. He would never make it off the mountain. Beck finally relented and joined a group of climbers, including Namba and climbing guide Neal Beidleman, in their descent.

Without his sight, Beck was tied to one end of a rope with the other end tied to the climber in front of him. The treachery of the descent without sight was incredibly dangerous. Beck slipped and fell numerous times, nearly dragging other climbers with him off the mountain. As they came within an hour's walk of the safety of the tents, a massive blizzard swelled around them, leaving them in complete whiteout conditions. The team was quickly disoriented in the storm, and with winds of more than one hundred miles an hour, there was clear danger of walking off the seven-thousand-foot vertical Kangshung Face to a certain death.

By this time, Beidleman knew they were lost and couldn't risk wandering blindly on the mountain. So he ordered the climbers to stop. Beck, Namba, and three other climbers would wait while Beidleman, Pete Schoening, and guide Mike Groom found the tents and sent back help.

Once they stopped climbing, Beck and the other climbers huddled in the relentless blizzard, shivering and freezing. Beidleman and the others made it to high camp. They collapsed exhausted in their tents after giving instructions to guide Anatoli Boukreev. Boukreev would bravely venture out into the blizzard several times before finding the group of half-dead climbers.

By the time Boukreev arrived, Namba had passed into unconsciousness, and Beck Weathers was unresponsive. Beck had inexplicably taken off his gloves and mask, and fallen face-first into the snow. Thinking Beck and Namba were too far gone, Boukreev helped the other climbers back to camp, leaving Beck for dead. In the morning, Beck's teammate Stuart Hutchinson found Namba and Beck lying next to each other in the snow. Beck was barely breathing. He was in a hypothermic coma. Every Everest climber knows that high up on the mountain there is no way to save someone in that condition. So Namba and Beck were, once again, left for dead.

When Hutchison returned to camp, team members radioed down to base camp, and the news was relayed to Peach back home in Dallas that Beck was dead. About four o'clock in the afternoon, however, twenty-two hours after the storm had stranded him and the others, a miracle occurred: Beck opened his eyes.

"At first I believed I was warm and comfortable in my bed at home," he said. "But as my head cleared, I saw my gloveless hand directly in front of my face, a gray and lifeless thing."

He slowly began to comprehend where he was, that he was alone on the mountain and no help was coming. If he was going to get off the mountain, it was entirely up to him. He struggled to his feet, dropped his pack, and determined that he would simply walk no matter what, and if he took a misstep and fell, so be it. He would keep moving until he fell down, couldn't walk anymore, or fell off the mountain.

Beck marched directly into the wind and miraculously found high camp. As he walked into camp half-dead, arms frozen stiff in front of his body, the climbers in camp couldn't believe their eyes! They called Peach to inform her that Beck wasn't quite as dead as they thought. In the hours and days that would follow, one miracle after another would get Beck off the mountain and into a hospital.

Beck would eventually lose both hands and parts of his face and feet to frostbite. He would endure numerous operations and reconstructive surgery. What were his feelings about his trip to Everest?

"People ask me whether I'd do it again," he said. "The answer is yes, even if I knew exactly everything that was going to happen to me on Mount Everest, I would do it again. That day on the mountain I traded my hands for my family and for my future . . . For the first time in my life I have peace."

It was a little less than two years after his return from Everest that I met Beck and Peach Weathers. It was an amazing experience for me. As we ate lunch and talked, they openly shared the troubles they had in their life and marriage before Beck's trip to Everest. They spoke of Beck's failure to give time to his marriage and family. Beck told me that God gave him a gift, an unspeakable gift: to open his eyes to what was most important.

Yes, Beck opened his physical eyes to get up and walk off the mountain. But God also opened his spiritual eyes to see how he could change and become the man he needed to be. He now views his wife, children, and life in an entirely different light.

While very few of us will ever stand atop Everest, we can still open our eyes to a new vision for our future. We don't need to travel to 29,029 feet to see what's important in life. But, like Beck Weathers, if we're not careful, we can get into the habit of living embedded in our obsessions and encompassed in our own warped way of viewing life.

1) You must open your eyes, and 2) no matter what the risk, you must walk in the direction of what you know you should do.

It's easy to let that happen. Worn down by the daily grind, we see our jobs as burdens, our children as trouble-prone, and life as endlessly difficult. We live far below our potential because we can't see a way off our mountain of troubles. If you're going to change your circumstances, two things that happened to Beck must happen to you: 1) you must open your eyes, and 2) no matter what the risk, you must walk in the direction of what you know you should do.

INSIGHTS FROM JAKE

I often get asked, "What are the most important things your fight with cancer has taught you?" Here's my answer:

1. **Put the Lord first in your life, above anything else, and draw strength from him.**

Life teaches all of us that circumstances will arise, some good and some bad. But God's foundation is unshakable. Putting God first puts all other things in the right perspective. Life's challenges aren't just things that happen with no intended meaning. They are purposeful and part of God's plan to teach us.

During my fight with cancer, there were many times I didn't feel like living life to its fullest, but through the strength of the Lord I was able to push through and keep my life normal. I held on to God's promises, as I knew he was holding on to me. When I went through chemotherapy and radiation treatments, I still played sports and practiced with the team. I went to school full-time and did my homework. I played golf and helped around the house. Leading up to my surgery to remove my remaining eye, I played football on my school team and competed in the play-off game five days after losing my sight. I was not going to let my lack of physical sight stop me.

2. **Love others and help those in need.**

My family, my friends, and my classmates have all been there for me. Because I felt the power of this love, I've developed a desire to help others. Maybe God gives us obstacles so we can see how important it is to have others to help us.

During many trips to the hospital, I couldn't help but see all the other children of all ages around me battling with other forms of disease. I couldn't meet many of them, but I often wondered if they were feeling love and support from others. So, even though I was only eight years old at the time, I decided to write a book so if any one of them didn't have someone to support them, they could read my book of hope and support. Many of the copies of my book ended up in Ronald McDonald houses across the country. To this day I give copies to children and adults in their time of need. I have also started a foundation that provides support to visually impaired children and raises funds to research the fight against cancer.

3. The only thing that stops you is you.

When I learned I was going to go blind, I decided I wasn't going to let it stop me in life or change my goals. Brokenness is not in the body; brokenness, where it exists, is in the mind, heart, or spirit. My mind, heart, and spirit remain whole. I thank God for that every day.

I've had moments of fear and worry, but my goals have not changed. They have only become more real. I have goals to remain an honor-roll student, positively impact others' lives, graduate from college, compete on the football field, and play competitive golf. I am pursuing these with a renewed level of energy and hope. In high school I have maintained a 4.4 grade point average. I went on a mission trip to Costa Rica. I play on my high school football team as a long-snapper. I just played a round of golf in the high 70s, and am practicing and improving my game every day. I started my Out of Sight Faith Foundation to raise money for other children.

What's on Your Belief Window?

According to author and CEO Hyrum Smith, we all have beliefs that act as our way of organizing our unique perception of the world. We form these beliefs throughout our lives. Some beliefs, however, are not based on reality. We make observations and draw conclusions that may or may not be true. Consider the person who believes he isn't capable or smart enough to reach a certain goal. It's easy to believe those thoughts when we are constantly living in self-pity or complaining that life isn't fair, but we are holding the wrong belief in front of our eyes. Our *belief window* is warped.

We all have windows through which we see the world and translate our perceptions. Each person's belief window contains statements of belief. This belief window can be changed and the statements rewritten. When we take out one pane and put another in our belief window, we view things differently. Psychologists call this *constructive development*. It's how we construct meaning or how we make meaning of things— trying on one belief and then another. We test these beliefs in our interactions with others until we arrive at a belief that reveals meaning in our life.

Jake Olson has constructed a clear and vibrant belief window. He sees things differently, not just because he has lost his physical sight, but because he has battled recurring cancer over and over again in his young life. He has stood atop the Everest of cancer. Jake could easily have "why me?" written across his belief window and view the world from the point of view of self-pity. But instead Jake takes the view of one blessed and fully equipped for life. With or without sight, with or without cancer, Jake's belief window allows him to see farther than his age or knowledge might otherwise extend, and endure all things with confidence.

There are time-tested principles that belong on our belief windows. Principles like forgiveness, integrity, faith, hope, and kindness. These principles are founded in truth. They don't change. In fact, when we place true principles on our belief window and act accordingly, we avoid mistakes and find more happiness. The right belief window also increases self-worth. With greater self-worth comes increased confidence in all areas of life. Likewise, when our actions conflict with the principles on our belief windows, we lose self-worth and confidence.

That's why trust in God can change you and your window to the world. Newfound faith from God's Word placed on your belief window creates a new way of living and making sense of life.

You Have to Decide

Not long ago, I met with a couple who had carelessly spent their way into serious debt. In fact, there was no way for them to make their debt payments with their income. They hadn't arrived in their situation overnight. It had taken years, but their habits were so established that they couldn't change their behavior quickly.

It started with small purchases on two credit cards. They rarely said no to things; saying yes became a habit. They decided to go on vacation to a beach resort. They knew they couldn't afford it, but they went anyway and charged the trip on both credit cards. When they returned, they were distraught. Their cards were maxed. It would take years to pay off the balance.

But rather than pay off the balance on those cards, they continued in their habitual behavior. Credit card companies sent them applications for new credit cards. With these new cards, they charged new furniture, electronics, clothing, and other items until they had more than fifty thousand dollars in credit card debt alone. In addition to their credit cards, they had car leases, a big mortgage, cell phone contracts, and much more.

They were depressed because of their situation. This affected their health and eating habits. They gained weight. Because of the stress, the husband got sick; soon he had missed too many days of work. His job was at risk. He had always been a top performer, but now he was likely to lose his job.

When we first sat down, we made a list of their income and expenses. We began to list ways to cut expenses. One of their expenses was premium service cable television at a cost of $98 per month. I crossed it out and wrote "$98/month" on the list of expense reductions. The husband immediately said, "Oh no. We can't cut cable television." I said, "Well, let's at least cut back to basic cable service, which costs $28 per month." He said, "No, that's just not possible."

We looked at his car payment. I told them they would have to sell his car and buy a less expensive car. This would save them $390 per month. Again, the husband wouldn't do it.

After going through a long list of expenses and repeating the dialogue again and again, we had only reduced their monthly expenses by a fraction of what was needed. I was about to give up when something inside the wife stirred, and she began to open her eyes. She encouraged her husband. She pleaded with him to sacrifice with her. I could see her rise up on top of her Everest and say, "No matter what, I'm walking off this mountain."

She asked me, "If we cut back on all the expenses you've listed and do what you ask, how long will it take to pay off these credit cards?"

I said, "If you do everything . . . three years."

"Then that's what we'll do," she said.

And that's exactly what they did. In fact, with their renewed sense of self-control, the husband started a part-time business that gave them the income they needed to get out of debt even faster. Now they not only live debt-free, but they also have more wisdom to live a happy life.

In Philippians 2, we're told to work out our salvation with fear and trembling. It also says something critical: "For it is God which worketh in you both to will and to do" (v. 13). When we set our vision (our "will") and our action ("to do") on what we need to change, God will give us the strength to make it happen.

It's amazing the rush of self-confidence and feelings of self-worth that come our way when we make even the smallest efforts to act in accordance with our beliefs. We begin to exercise what psychologists call *self-authorship,* or the ability to direct our own behavior rather than having our behavior dictated by our circumstances. Living a self-authored life is enlightening.

The apostle Paul experienced this rush of enlightenment, as it says in Acts 9:18, "And immediately there fell from his eyes as it had been scales: and he received sight forthwith, and arose, and was baptized." When we move in the direction of what we know to be right, it's as if scales drop from in front of our eyes and we begin to see things as they really are. We can then break our inertia and act with confidence.

Once we see things in a new way, we must begin to move in the direction we know we should. In Romans 7, the apostle Paul said, "For to will is present with me; but how to perform that which is good I find not" (v. 18). We may be willing but unable to act because we don't know how. Ironically, we often discover the *how* only after we start acting. If we pause, never acting, the how is not made clear to us. That's why taking action, even in small ways, can help you open your eyes, see how to change, and give you the confidence to move forward and escape your Everest.

Let's consider the addict who is consumed with an addiction. He can't escape it. He can't see how to change. But if he starts to act in small ways (physical exercise, prayer, giving service to others, putting himself in places where he can feed his mind with positive things), these small things lead to bigger actions that can lead to an escape from the addiction itself.

A Break*through* Requires a Break *With*

Someone once said, "If you want to hear the sound of your own accent, listen to your kids talk." We pass on more than our accent or eye color to our children, and those habits aren't always positive. Any parent knows that many of his or her habits get passed on to the next generation. Likewise, many of us have picked up a few habits from our parents that we wish hadn't been passed down our family line.

The *American Journal of Public Health* reports that depression is a familial disorder resulting from genetic and environmental influences.[1] While genetics aren't the only cause of depression, it serves to illustrate that we have inherited behaviors and traits from our parents.

We often hear people say, "I got my impatience from my mother" or "I drive like my father." If we look closely at the areas of our lives where we struggle, we may see that our families have passed on to us weaknesses we don't want. But just because our weaknesses didn't originate with us, it doesn't mean we need to persist in them or pass them on to the next generation.

> If negative patterns exist in your life, you can break the cycle and be an agent for change in your family.

If negative patterns exist in your life, you can break the cycle and be an agent for change in your family. Whether it's a pattern of divorce, addiction, criticism, or negative thinking, don't use it as an excuse to continue the behavior. Instead, do something about it. The pattern can stop with you.

What is your Everest? Have you struggled with a weakness so long that you wonder if you'll ever get off the mountain? If you're feeling that way, you're not alone. Rest assured, God will help you open your eyes. You can stand up and walk to a new life. You might lose a few things in the process; it might not be a hand or foot, like Beck Weathers, but you'll likely have to sacrifice something to reach your end goal.

Jesus said, "If thy right eye offend thee, pluck it out, and cast it from thee: for it is profitable for thee that one of thy members should perish and not that thy whole body should be cast into hell" (Matt. 5:29). Maybe you'll have to give up shopping to get out of debt, lose certain friends to be around positive people, spend your time being with your children more often, or sacrifice leisure so you can exercise and be more physically fit. Whatever the sacrifice, you can begin today.

Jake's doctors knew that in order to preserve his life, his remaining eye would have to be taken. Jake and his parents gave up his sight in order to keep his life. But God has blessed Jake with more than sight.

INSIGHTS FROM BRIAN

In early September 2009, during a checkup visit, the doctor found that a small tumor had come back in Jake's eye. Later that same week, with Jake under anesthesia, the doctor went in to examine the eye up close and saw several small tumors developing. When he came out of the surgery room to tell us the news, Cindy immediately started crying, as she knew this news would probably lead to the removal of Jake's remaining eye. Jake was unable to go through any additional radiation. Removal was the only alternative to stop the cancer and save his life. We asked the doctor to treat it with the cryotherapy and laser light treatment anyway, in hopes a miraculous recovery could occur.

We sat there and cried for an hour or two before Jake awoke from the anesthesia. We prayed. We pulled it together as much as we could. Right then was not the time to tell him about the tumors; he was just waking up from the procedure. Besides, we were awaiting a final call from the doctors later in the day to see if they could find any additional course of action. Maybe, just maybe, there was something else the doctors would propose. We had been through every kind of treatment possible.

When Jake awoke, we squeezed his hand, kissed his forehead, and spoke to him, just letting him know we were there. We had gone through this countless times: all the checkups under anesthesia, the laser treatments, the cryo treatments, the arterial chemo treatments, and the catho-port procedures. The return squeeze of his hand let us know he was okay. Despite the number of treatments, we were always grateful when Jake came out of anesthesia successfully. Every time Jake was wheeled into the operating room, our hearts wept. Then there was always the waiting, pacing, watching of the second hand on the clock tick, and the prayers. When Jake woke up this day, we got him ready, called for the wheelchair, got him to the car, and went to Red Robin, Jake's favorite restaurant.

Everyone has their comfort food. For some it's coffee; for others it's chocolate. For Jake, it's Red Robin! He loves the root beer floats, the tower of onion rings, a salad with ranch dressing, and a burger—no cheese, just lettuce, tomato, and ketchup. After every trip to the hospital over the last eight or nine years, we made a habit of stopping at Red Robin. We probably visited this particular Red Robin one hundred times, and we became accustomed to the routine. The stop on that September day after the procedure, however, was far from typical. Usually Red Robin would cheer us up, but not this day. It was a painful, sorrowful, empty day.

All morning we cried in disbelief. We were still crying at the table at Red Robin; we just didn't have tears coming down. Watching our son sip his root beer, we reflected on the preciousness of our children and the love we have for them.

The waiter returned with the onion rings and our drinks. We were sick inside and didn't feel like eating. There was nothing we could do. This was real life. You aren't trained for this stuff. These are the moments you find out what kind of person you are. You find the strength.

Jake remained home that afternoon and recuperated. Emma had a basketball game, and I attended. On the way home, I began sharing some things with Emma, but not the whole story. That would have to come later that night when we sat down with Jake. At some point during the drive home, I received a frantic call from Cindy, saying that I needed to get there as soon as possible.

"Brian, get home fast," she said.

"What's wrong?" I asked. "Is Jake okay?"

"No," she said, "he's not. I received a call back from the hospital and Jake overheard the conversation. He knows. I didn't even get a chance to prepare him first."

"I'll be there as fast as I can," I told her.

"Hurry!"

As Cindy was talking to the doctor on the phone, Jake had overheard parts of the conversation and figured out his fate.

Jake's initial reaction was guttural. He screamed, "I don't want to be blind! It's not fair! I fought so hard for so long and now cancer somehow wins. This sucks!" Jake knew that in order to preserve his life, his eye would have to go. But that's a hard thing for a twelve-year-old boy to accept. He was angry and scared.

When we got home, everyone sat and cried even though we were too weak to cry anymore. There was not much to say. I guess the tears said it all. I assured everyone that we would stay strong and we would get through this. For some reason though, right at the moment of discouragement, I had an impression. A deep-down inner belief took root that Jake was just "going to soar." It had to be a message from God, because in that moment my mind was not working on its own.

The impression was accompanied by a sense of freedom and peace. Jake was going to soar. Any remaining chains would be off our boy, and the sky was going to be the limit. It was our heavenly Father letting me know that this would somehow work out.

Every evening we say prayers together as a family. Jake draws on this for comfort. He uses the time to talk not only to God, but also to Cindy and me. After prayers that night, Jake began talking.

"Maybe the worst part," he started, "is that I will no longer be able to see your faces."

He just started crying. Cindy and I started crying. We hugged him and told him we heard what he just said. You can't very well say we understood, because one can't. We couldn't tell him it was going to be all right, because it didn't seem to fit. We just had to listen to him. Jake talked about not being able to see Emma and other family members, his friends at school, and his teachers. He had concerns about doing normal things, things any twelve-year-old loves to do. We continued to cry.

Jake is so personable. He loves people and friends, his dogs and his home. His surroundings are very important to him. It just didn't seem fair that this was happening. Not to Jake. Not to any child. Jake didn't reach any particular conclusion that evening. He wanted to sleep between Mom and Dad. We said a final prayer and kissed good night.

It seems that too often we live below our aspirations and then begin to accept the lives we're living. What's holding you back in life? Whatever it is, change what's on your belief window. You can do it. You can prevent your weaknesses from being passed on to the next generation. You can begin in small ways to make a difference in your life. Open your eyes. Come down off your Everest and live the life God intended for you to live.

> To experience the happiness of true change, you'll have to break with prior habits, see things in a new way, and do something about it.

It's time for you to soar. If you're weary of dealing with bad habits, or burdened with something you've struggled with for a long time, now is the time to break through, leave it behind, and make a change. Even though it's painful, change can lead to a happy end. Open your eyes to the possibilities before you.

Maybe you've struggled with expressing your feelings to your spouse. Perhaps your family didn't express love, and it's just not some-thing you do very well. Can you see how you could bless the lives of those around you if you could change? Every break*through* requires a break *with*. To experience the happiness of true change, you'll have to break with prior habits, see things in a new way, and do something about it.

In Summary

- Open your eyes and take steps to change when conquering your Everest.
- Change what's on your belief window and act on true principles.
- Take action, even in small ways, to begin changing and improving.
- Be a blessing to future generations by making good decisions today.

LEMONS AND MOLEHILLS

*Flops are a part of life's menu, and I've never been
a girl to miss out on any of the courses.*

—ROSALIND RUSSELL

For eight decades, a landmark study has been under way at Harvard University. The participants in this study, who were students and young adults in the 1920s, were interviewed and given health exams throughout their lives to determine what factors lead to health and happiness. The results revealed things the researchers didn't anticipate. In fact, they revealed the secret to living a happy life.

Longitudinal studies such as the Harvard study are the most difficult to conduct, but they yield the richest information. A typical research study takes a measurement at a single point in time, a cross-section of data. But longitudinal studies use repeated observations of the same subjects over long periods of time—often decades. They follow the same cohort (a group of like-kind people) over a lifetime to see the actual cumulative results.

If you want to see the true impact of poverty, follow poor children into their adult years. If you want to see the impact of being a twin, follow sets of twins for a lifetime. But because of the cost and logistics involved, very few in-depth longitudinal studies are ever conducted.

The Study of Adult Development at Harvard University has followed and studied three cohorts of men and women since the 1920s:

- The Harvard Cohort—a sample of 268 socially advantaged Harvard graduates born around 1920
- The Inner City Cohort—made up of 456 Boston youths sent to reform school, and 500 boys who at age 14 hadn't been in reform school
- The Terman Women Cohort—a 1922 selection of Californian school-aged children with IQs of over 140

Participants in these studies were interviewed and given a physical exam every two to five years. The study not only examined physical health but also tracked a host of other factors in an attempt to determine what caused or detracted from the developmental, emotional, and mental health of the participants.

The study revealed causes of good or poor health. Interestingly, ancestral longevity, cholesterol, or stress didn't determine the quality of health beyond age fifty in the lives of the participants. Rather, smoking, alcohol, weight, and exercise were the highest predictors of whether someone would be healthy. While smoking was the biggest contributor to poor health, exercise was the leveling factor. Consistent exercise led to greater health despite other harmful factors. Even for those who were overweight, if they included regular exercise in their lives, they had significantly improved health and longevity.

While health was one emphasis of the study, the most surprising results came when researchers discovered what factors led to happiness in life. At first glance, one would think the Harvard Cohort, with average incomes of more than $105,000 during their working years and high social standing, would be happier because of their wealth or circumstances. Or one might think than the Inner City Cohort, with average incomes of below $35,000, would reveal that poverty leads to unhappiness. You would think the Terman women, with IQs of over 140, would make more intelligent life choices and have better health and longevity. But the study revealed that neither income nor IQ were significant factors in determining happiness. As the research progressed and the participants aged, other factors began to emerge.

Like all of us, the study participants made choices, some of them bad choices. They also had bad things happen to them in life that were beyond their control. Over time, researchers observed it's not the bad things that happen to us that determine our happiness, but what we choose to do with those things. In fact, some of the happiest individuals in the study made bad choices or suffered devastating illness and loss during their lifetimes. The bad experiences themselves weren't a predictor of happiness or unhappiness. For almost all participants who were rated as happy, their poor choices or circumstances set up their next successful steps in life. Rather than setbacks, they used their failures as setups to living the rest of their lives more happily and successfully.

Researchers in the study call this "adaptive coping style" and describe it as the "capacity to turn lemons into lemonade and not to turn molehills into mountains."[1] This positive adaptation to life played a significantly greater role than genetics, wealth, race, or other factors in determining how happy people were later in life. It isn't so much what they started with, what mistakes they made, or what happened to them that influenced their happiness in life; it's what they did with what happened to them that made all the difference!

One study participant, Bill Graham, suffered years of abuse as a child. Researchers described his early years as filled with "starvation, abuse, lack of love and aloneness."[2] His mother gave him up to foster care when he was three and a half years old. When Bill was six, his father was committed to a state hospital for psychosis. He was beaten by his foster parents. He said, "I always knew someone was coming to visit because I got fed and cleaned."

In the researchers' scoring system, only 16 of the 456 Inner City Cohort suffered worse childhoods than Bill. Amazingly, in subsequent research visits, researchers observed that Bill went on to mold a rich and happy life for himself.

Graham married well. His wife was "unselfish, kind, loving, and generous." She was dependable and considerate. She was devoted to him, and they created a family of their own. His life became immensely satisfying. In a gesture of incredible charity, he took in his father, the same man who had neglected him as a child, out of the "inhumane conditions of the state hospital" to live with him. During the lonely, isolated final years of her life, he regularly visited the mother who had placed him in foster care.

> "Learn to live in thankfulness, looking back at what you have had, and at what you didn't have but that you do have now."

Then, at age fifty-three, Graham suffered a devastating blow. His wife died of cancer. Her death was overwhelming for him. He was hospitalized for major depression. But that isn't where his story ends. At age fifty-eight, five years after his wife's death, Graham found a new mission in life: helping others who suffered as he did. He went on to create a ministry. He teaches how to live a life of peace. He ministers to the sick, helping them feel safe and comfortable. He remarried and found greater spiritual purpose in life. Researchers rated him in their highest happiness category despite his being stricken by bladder cancer, kidney failure, and triple bypass heart surgery. Graham said, "Learn to live in thankfulness, looking back at what you have had, and at what you didn't have but that you do have now."[3]

As Longfellow wrote, "Thy fate is the common fate of all, / Into each life some rain must fall, / Some days must be dark and dreary."[4] But just as the researchers from the Harvard study learned, it isn't what happens to us that matters; it's what we do with what happens to us that makes all the difference.

INSIGHTS FROM JAKE

When setbacks come my way, I try to focus on the positives. I try to decide right from the get-go that it isn't going to stop me. This includes golf. Perhaps setbacks in golf are not on the same level as fighting cancer, but you can learn a lot from them.

Sometimes I will go out to the range on a Tuesday after a weekend of great golf and find myself hitting poorly. When something is off, it's frustrating. When that happens, I get back to center, slow down, feel my swing, and focus on the details of my swing. I become very thoughtful and deliberate. And the thoughtfulness generally allows me to understand the underlying reasons for the poor shots and allows me to make adjustments. It can be a simple thing, and *bam*—I have my swing back and the balls are flying straight. It becomes a game of tempo, calm, and temperament. It's a dance. There are days that the dance just doesn't work, and I need to leave it and come back the next day. But I know I will get it and correct it, and be a better golfer for it.

The same thing happens in life. Sometimes your swing in life is off. But when you get back to center, slow down, and are deliberate, you improve.

Discover a New Way of Thinking

In 2006, I led a large-scale adult development research study among adults in the United States and Canada to determine the factors that led them to, among other things, social and emotional maturity. One of the major findings from the study was that many adults get "stuck" as a result of their failures. They become so caught up and embedded in their failures that they can't find a way out. For example, some people go through divorce and emerge having learned valuable lessons, thereby making better marriage choices later in life. They seem to have the wherewithal to keep the wisdom gained but shrug off the mistake itself.

Others, however, never get over the hurt, emotional scarring, or need to retaliate. They vow never to get themselves into such a painful situation again. They begin to relate to most things in life through the perspective of their bad marriage. They say things like, "Since my divorce, I've been—" or "My ex-husband doesn't think I can—" They see life through the lens of their past. This way of thinking wasn't limited to divorce. I studied many adults who were stuck in life for other reasons. Personality conflicts, habits, addictions, and an unwillingness to move beyond their way of thinking kept some adults from becoming the people they want to become. Overwhelmingly, those who couldn't emerge from their situations felt like failures and let it define them and their futures.

So how do you learn from failure in life without feeling like a failure? How can you emerge from life's setbacks and set up a way to move forward? In the adult development study, adults who moved forward had two things the others didn't have: 1) a mentor or friend who helped them move beyond the failure, and 2) a source of inspiration that elevated their vision of who they could become.

When emotionally mature adults find themselves embedded in a temporary failure or setback, they have the capability to stand back and view themselves and their situations as if they are looking through a camera. They can think about and describe their own behavior as if they were independent from themselves. They can see without bias what they need to do differently. They are objective, not subjective about their behavior. One study participant who moved beyond a divorce said, "I took a step back and thought, 'Why did I settle?' I got married because all my friends were getting married. I can see how I let myself get into a situation I didn't want to be in."

When we step back and assess our situations, it gives us the ability to *choose* what to do with what's happened to us. However, it's very difficult to step away from our embedded-ness and view our lives from this perspective alone. That's why we need someone to help us. For example, the divorcee who successfully failed forward had a father who helped her through her thought process and supported her unconditionally. He helped her see things clearly. He was patient and helped her see her way through.

In addition to a mentor or friend, study participants who failed forward had a source of ongoing inspiration. For some, it was a deeper connection with God. Scripture was key for them. For others, it was inspiration from good books or uplifting messages in their daily reading. One of the key conclusions from the study is that when we combine the learning we gain from life's mistakes with ongoing reading and inspiration, we are more likely to overcome and fail forward. Why? We give ourselves a new pattern of thinking.

> When we combine the learning we gain from life's mistakes with ongoing reading and inspiration, we are more likely to overcome and fail forward.

Our brains are constantly organizing information. Our brains automatically take what happens to us, even complex input like feelings, and store that information in a way that allows us to make sense of it. Because of the enormous complexity of life, our brains store and retrieve information differently from one person to another. It's been described as being more like a series of improvisations by a jazz musician than the playing of a piece of written music by a classical musician.

As a result, our minds store and retrieve information from a conglomerate of input organized by what we constantly think about. What we think about is our frame of reference. Our brains use what we constantly think about as a catalog system for input and retrieval. For example, if a child has been verbally abused, when he interacts with other children his brain likely tries to fit the images and feelings of interacting with others into his prevailing framework, which was formed based on verbal abuse. His way of relating to the world was framed by his way of relating at home. As a result, he may act out in ways perceived as antisocial or inappropriate. His catalog system never lets him move beyond his abuse; he is constantly reminded of it.

As adults we're no different. If following a divorce, we replay in our minds the reasons we're unattractive, angry, or full of feelings of mistrust, then our brains begin to create a frame of reference based on those thoughts and feelings. New input from life gets cataloged for future reference based on feelings of mistrust or trust. After that, we begin to relate to people based on our mistrust for them rather than other, more healthy ways. When we do, we shut out other ways of interacting with people, narrow our way of thinking, create impressions that may not be based on reality, and limit our relationships in the future.

When we are in the midst of failure, we need to give our brains a framework based on true principles and lasting ways of categorizing our experiences. If we're not reading, listening, or feeding our brains new, positive external sources of thought, our brains use our preoccupation with our failures as the map for storing and retrieving information. However, if we're feeding our minds with thoughts and ideas that give us hope, if we feed our brains the idea that we can overcome, then those are the thoughts that will be recalled and used.

This concept is called *anchoring*. When our brains don't have a well-defined basis for making a decision, they rely on whatever information is available. We then use that information as the beginning point for making sense of our experiences. When our way of thinking is anchored in true principles, in hope, or in the possibility of becoming better, then all future thoughts come and go in our brains based on that framework.

That's why a trusted mentor or friend can help us talk through life's challenges and face life's failures with better perspective. That's why using God's framework as our framework allows us to think like him. We aren't relying on our own embedded frames of reference.

When we make reading uplifting words a daily undertaking, we constantly structure our frame of reference in new, positive ways, thereby giving ourselves the ability to react to failure the right way. Armed with this way of thinking, we can guide our lives when we encounter life's setbacks. We anchor our way of thinking to true and uplifting principles.

Remember: It's Halftime

Thank heaven games don't end at halftime! If they did, the record books would be written differently. If Super Bowl XLIV, between the Indianapolis Colts and the New Orleans Saints, had ended at halftime, the Colts would have won and the city of New Orleans, struggling to emerge from hurricane devastation, wouldn't have had a victory to boost the city's morale and image.

If games ended at halftime, the famous battle between Dallas and Pittsburgh in Super Bowl X would have ended in a victory for Dallas rather than the thrilling victory to Pittsburgh and the famous long bomb to Lynn Swann.

Halftime is perhaps the most important part of the game. What do teams do at halftime? They review what worked and what didn't work. They make adjustments and new plans for doing things better in the second half. They get inspired. They get refreshed and prepared now that they are more familiar with their opponent. They use what they've learned to go out and play better.

Life is very much the same. We can step aside, go into the locker room, and assess how we're doing at life. Now we're more familiar with our opponent, we can make adjustments and get refreshed to begin anew. At halftime, there isn't anything you can do about the first half's score. It's done. It's in the record books. At halftime, you can't spend any time wishing things were different. You can only take what you've learned and make urgent plans for change. Life's halftime is the same. The more time spent on the new game plan, the better we'll be.

Learning from our lives is what we were meant to do. So get over your past failures. They're in the record books. We can only control what we choose to do today. This means we need to stop focusing on what's happened and focus instead on what's going to happen.

> **We need to act, not react, our way to success.**

When we fail, we often react in unproductive ways. We get angry or depressed, cover up our mistakes, ignore our mistakes, relive our failures over and over again, or simply give up. These are reactions rather than actions. We need to act, not react, our way to success.

Think about the coach of a game. Imagine if a coach's reaction to mistakes in the first half was to be depressed. Can you see a coach reliving and reviewing the mistake over and over again? Can you see him sitting in the locker room, head in hands, wondering why bad things always happen to him? If he reacted like this, he wouldn't have time to get a new game plan or focus on what's next. A good coach knows there is a second half to be played and it's not won or lost on a single play. So, he keeps his head in the game and prepares for the next half.

If you're facing a setback, remember, it's halftime. Get your game plan written down. Decide your course of action. Your written plan will guide you from feeling like a failure to moving forward as a result of the failure.

Don't Make Mountains out of Molehills

It's often the little frustrations in life that cause the biggest problems. It seems as if when a big crisis appears, we rise to the occasion and handle it with courage and grace. But the small frustrations ignite the worst in us. Someone once coined the phrase "Don't make mountains out of molehills." Molehills are small mounds of dirt left when a mole digs a hole in the ground. We make mountains from molehills when we blow things out of proportion or overreact to the small inconveniences that come our way. If we get delayed in traffic or the children leave a mess in the kitchen, we tend to overreact, and we give away our power to be happy.

Recently a man I knew bought a new $80,000 European car. It was a beautiful car. It had gorgeous leather seats, and the interior was stunning. The car was fast, fuel-efficient, and had every bell and whistle a person could want. After having the car for a week, he noticed that the heated seats were slow to heat up. Every time he got in the car, he was frustrated that the heated seats were so slow. He complained about it all the time. He couldn't drive the car without thinking about it.

Finally, he traded in the beautiful car, lost more than $10,000 on his trade, and bought another car just because he was frustrated with the heated seats. The funny thing was he later learned the switch in his European car worked backward from the American-made cars he had owned, and each time he thought he was turning up his heated seats, he was actually turning them down. He gave up a beautiful car that he loved in every other respect because he couldn't stop focusing on one small issue.

We do the same with people. We can focus so long on someone's shortcomings that we can't see all the other wonderful qualities that person possesses. If we focus on what we don't like about someone, we soon reach the point where we can't see anything good in him or her at all. Many couples fall in love only to fall out of love because one or both cannot look past the small things inherent in the other's personality or actions. They even start to resent each other as a result.

When we get into the habit of focusing on the small things others do that irritate us, we also overlook our own faults and misgivings. We can be so focused on another person's problem that we forget we have even bigger problems to solve. Making mountains out of molehills is selfish thinking. When we get into the habit of focusing on another person's small problems, he or she senses our disapproval. Soon, mistrust and divisive thinking can enter into the relationship.

The truth is, God wants us to be different. Notice that no one looks exactly the same. We have different features, and we come in all shapes and sizes. It's our differences that allow us to learn from each other and grow. Imagine what a boring place our world would be if we were all the same. In fact, we were made different so we could teach each other important lessons that we wouldn't learn otherwise. So celebrate the differences in other people instead of complaining about them.

When we make mountains from molehills, we expect others to change, when it may be we who need to change. Isn't it ironic that the person who needs to learn patience is blessed with a spouse who is always running late? That the person who needs to learn humility is blessed with a friend who overachieves? It's not irony. It's God blessing us with what we need to learn. What if we were to focus on what we need to learn rather than what *they* need to fix? Would we be happier? You bet. We'd have less stress, argument, and ill feelings.

How do you learn to value and appreciate the differences in others? Exaggerate the good in them. Magnify what they do well. When you constantly think about what you appreciate in another person, you can't see the small problems. Remarkably, he or she notices our approval and encouragement, and wants to become better as a result. When we love others and encourage them, they try harder to work on their small quirks and peculiarities.

It may be these mountains—the mountains we make from molehills—that faith can move. The Lord said that with even the smallest faith, that of a mustard seed, we could move mountains (Matt. 17:20). When we exaggerate the bad in others, we make mountains out of molehills. But we can move those mountains when we have faith in our loved ones. When we magnify their strengths, we faithfully remove the mountains that stand in their way.

Rather than criticizing those who are different, what if we found humor in our differences? When we do, we bring flavor into life. Imagine cooking your favorite chili recipe without any spices whatsoever. It would be bland. The same goes with life. When we see, appreciate, and find joy in each other's small differences, we find the richness in life. We can lighten up. We can let things go that don't matter. We can leave it alone. When we laugh at our differences, the laughter seems to sweep up the tension or anxiety and remove it from our lives. Humor works.

We often treat ourselves the same way we treat others. We focus on our small problems. We exaggerate our weaknesses. As a result, we're overly stressed and critical. We lose our happiness. When we view our challenges from God's perspective, however, we see that what we thought was a big deal really wasn't that big of a deal at all. We see that time has a way of fixing most things.

Let the small things go. Find humor in the variation and diversity of life. Value small missteps; they make us better. Don't sweat the small stuff. Go with the flow.

INSIGHTS FROM JAKE

The most discouraging days for me are those when something happens to remind me I'm not independent. It's when I can't figure something out on the computer and have to ask for help.

In a crowded hallway at school, I often run into people. I apologize and they apologize, but it's frustrating because I can't see them coming. Even brushing my teeth can be frustrating because when you can't see your toothbrush, sometimes you end up putting too much paste on your brush, sometimes too little, and sometimes none at all!

Imagine if I let every little thing that happens to me because I can't see get me down. I would be constantly discouraged. I can't focus on those things. I'm happier when I focus on what I'm doing well. I am independent in so many ways. I look forward to another day when I can learn to do something new. I throw the football with my dad. Sometimes I miss by a long ways, but sometimes I throw it right into his hands. That's pretty good for someone who can't see where he's throwing. I have also learned to long snap a football when in punt or field goal formation. I am on my high school varsity football team and have used my skills as a center to apply them to long snapping the football.

Don't Give In to Criticism

It's not always our mistakes that keep us from moving forward in life. Criticism can be crippling. When others criticize us, it can feel like we've failed. Truth be told, we don't cause many of the challenges we face in life. Most challenges are created by other people. We've all experienced criticism, sometimes fairly and other times unfairly. Whether at the hand of a family member, friend, or work associate, we've all felt criticism's biting sting.

But all feedback, critical or not, can work to our benefit. The trick to thriving with criticism is deciding which criticism is useful and which isn't. We all have the natural tendency to get defensive when someone criticizes us or our performance. But if we let down our defenses, can we decipher the valuable feedback from the fictional?

What about unfair criticism, gossip, or malicious comments that come your way? How do you avoid letting them affect you? The answer is simple: always be true to others outside their presence. Never criticize them. When we are criticized, our first tendency is to lash out. But instead of going directly to the person who offended us, we'll often spend time telling someone else, such as our spouse or a friend, just how rotten the person is who criticized us. We justify, stew, get angry, and imagine retaliation. But all of that is wasted time and effort.

When we're true to others outside their presence, we say nothing but good about them. What about those who have spoken ill of us? Be especially true to them. Say only good things about them. There is extremely positive energy created inside our hearts and minds when we choose to follow the scripture that says, "Do good to them that . . . despitefully use you, and persecute you" (Matt. 5:44). Think about the peace that would come to your life if every time you have been criticized you chose the high road.

One of my favorite stories of criticism is about Mildred, who was the lead gossiper at her church and the self-appointed monitor of the church's morals. Mildred had the nasty habit of sticking her nose into other people's business.

Many of the people who attended church with Mildred didn't approve of her "extracurricular" activities, but feared her enough to maintain their silence. Mildred made a mistake, however, when she accused George, a new member of the congregation, of being an alcoholic after she saw his old pickup parked in front of the town's only bar one afternoon.

She emphatically told George in front of a group of churchgoers that everyone in town would know what he was doing when they saw his truck sitting there in front of the local tavern. "They'll know exactly what you're doing!" she told him.

George, a man of few words, stared at her for a moment and then turned and walked away. He didn't explain, defend, or deny anything. He kept his silence. Later that evening, George drove his pickup across town, quietly parked it in front of Mildred's house, and left it there all night!

Why do we let other people upset us so easily? It's always been surprising to me the anger exhibited once we get behind the wheel of a moving vehicle. We can be driving down the road, make an error in driving, and immediately get an obscene gesture from another driver. More amazing is that we'll be upset for the rest of the day. We don't even know the person!

> "Give and it shall be given unto you; good measure, pressed down, and shaken together, and running over, shall men give into your bosom." (Luke 6:38)

Why do we do this? Because we are social creatures and we value what others think. But if we're not careful, we can let other people's opinions of us take over and control our lives. We can't please everyone. It's that simple. No matter how hard you try in life, you cannot make everyone happy. So run your own race. Stop trying to please the critics. Not everyone is going to understand you.

Remember, we can return kindness regardless of what others do to us. As Scripture says, "Give and it shall be given unto you; good measure, pressed down, and shaken together, and running over, shall men give into your bosom" (Luke 6:38). We can be a friend to those who are not friendly. We can seek out ways to make others smile. We can be an instrument in God's hands for doing good to others. We can push criticism out of our lives by embracing its opposite: encouragement.

INSIGHTS FROM JAKE

God put us here on earth not only to develop a relationship with him but also to share him with others and to help each other. God tells us to love everyone.

I have been blessed to receive help and love from so many people and friends. On the last day of school before I went blind, at my request all the junior high students dressed up in formal clothes and threw a party for me. We prayed together, we danced, and everyone looked wonderful. One of my teachers even wore her wedding dress that day. I had told my principal that I wanted to remember everyone dressed up. It was wonderful! I will always be able to hold these images in my mind of how nice they looked. My school, my classmates, and my friends have been supportive and loving toward me. It has been a blessing.

Throughout my battle with cancer, my friends have always been there for me. This includes giving me encouraging messages that made me feel like they were there no matter what happened. For instance, on one occasion when I was in fourth grade and knew I was going into the hospital for a surgery and a lengthy stay, my entire fourth grade class surprised me with a pillow case with their names, pictures, sports stuff, and some encouraging notes on them. It made me feel loved and gave me comfort and courage. One of the notes was from my friend Evan. It said:

> Dear Jake,
>
> Angels are watching over you, even the baseball team [I'm a Los Angeles Angels fan]. I am praying for you every night so you can come back to school and play football with Connor and me.
>
> Your friend, Evan

And then my friend Connor wrote me the following:

Dear Jake,

See you on Wednesday. I want you to be strong and do well in chemo. You're the best! Please get better and remember the Lord is with you.

Love, Connor

P.S. Good luck and feel better. I miss you.

Emma wrote to me:

Jake,

Get well soon, I'm praying for you.

Love, Emma

On another occasion, I was heading from California to New York City for a special surgery to inject a chemo drug through my leg artery, up my entire body for direct injection into my eye. This was an experimental treatment and it had risks. I was scared, and I was most concerned about having to lie still for eight hours after the surgery. I shared this with my classmates. My fifth-grade class recorded a series of messages, songs, and jokes on a recorder so I could listen to them while recovering from the treatment. They presented it to me the day before my departure to New York. All this really helped me through my treatments and my battle with cancer.

> Take criticism, use the part that's valuable, be true to others, and remember you can't please everyone.

Kindness can move mountains. When you receive constructive criticism from others, thank them. A heartfelt "thank you" will do as much for you as for them. Once you've thanked them, remember you don't have to fix everything at once. Don't let someone's criticism take you off your game plan. Be content working on what's most important. That means you may disappoint a few people along the way. Take criticism, use the part that's valuable, be true to others, and remember you can't please everyone. Then you'll be able to move forward despite any criticism that comes your way.

Turn on your adaptive coping style. Make lemonade out of lemons. Don't make mountains out of molehills. Learn from your mistakes. We can choose to respond to our setbacks in a positive and optimistic way. We can discover a new way of thinking.

In Summary

- View a temporary failure as an opportunity to get better.
- When we feed our minds positive and inspiring thoughts, we frame our way of thinking in ways that can make us happy.
- Don't make mountains out of molehills.
- Don't give in to criticism. Always be true and encouraging to others.

5

THE WINNER WITHIN

I am the greatest, I said that even before I knew I was.

—MUHAMMAD ALI

T hat was the first time I was ever scared in the ring," Muhammad Ali said. "Sonny Liston. First time. First round. Said he was gunna kill me."[1]

Sonny Liston was a brutal boxer and ex-convict known for his toughness, punching power, and intimidating appearance. He was viciously mean, his managers were mobsters, and he gained his hard-hitting fighting skills in prison. In the late 1950s, Liston vanquished fighter after fighter as he plowed his way to the top of the rankings, defeating most opponents by knockout, using his brutal toughness to intimidate everyone. Henry Cooper's manager, Jim Wicks, said, "We don't even want to meet Liston walking down the same street," and refused to schedule a fight with him.

In 1962, Liston had trampled his way to the top and was waiting for heavyweight champion Floyd Patterson, who finally consented to fight him. The fight was scheduled for New York, but because of Liston's prison record and mob connections, New York denied him license. So the fight was moved to Illinois.

Patterson was the reigning Olympic champion. He was agile and smooth, nothing like Liston, who relied almost exclusively on his size and power. In 1956, at the age of twenty-one, Patterson had become the youngest heavyweight champion ever when he won the champion's belt against Archie Moore. He was boxing's golden boy with an almost flawless fighting record.

Despite Patterson's record, his fight with Liston lasted only a matter of minutes. Liston knocked him out in the first round. Patterson asked for a rematch in 1963 and the outcome was no different, with Liston knocking him out in the first round again, only this time ten seconds slower than the first.

Waiting in the wings for Liston the following year was the up-and-coming Cassius Clay. Clay was a glib, fast-talking, twenty-two-year-old challenger who enjoyed the spotlight. He had won the light-heavy-weight gold medal at the 1960 Rome Olympics. Clay had great hand and foot speed—not to mention a limitless supply of self-confidence. In the previous year, however, he was almost knocked out by southpaw Henry Cooper. As a result, he was thought to be too soft for a brutal fighter such as Liston. No one thought Clay would make it past the first round. The *Los Angeles Times'* Jim Murray observed, "The only thing at which Clay can beat Liston is reading the dictionary."[2] Leading up to the fight, Clay was a seven-to-one underdog.

The bout was scheduled for February 25, 1964, in Miami Beach. In the days and weeks leading up to the fight, Clay unrelentingly forecasted his victory. He insisted to a skeptical press that he would knock out Liston in eight rounds. For all the prefight talk, Clay would later admit, deep down, he was worried.

At the start of the fight, many of the fans in attendance were surprised to see that Liston was shorter than Clay. Clay took advantage of his height and, in the first round, used his fast jab as his major weapon, followed by quick flurries of combinations. He darted in and out, avoiding Liston's heavy punches. By the third round, Clay had opened up a cut under Liston's left eye.

After the sixth round, an exhausted and demoralized Liston told his corner that he couldn't continue. When the bell rang for the seventh round, Liston sat in his corner. Clay was declared winner by technical knockout. Immediately, he began to dance in the center of the ring. In one of the most famous scenes in sports history, to be replayed over and over throughout the years, Clay yelled, "I'm the greatest!" and "I shook up the world!"

No doubt about it, Muhammad Ali (to which Clay changed his name shortly thereafter) was a winner. He would prove it again in the ring in a well-publicized rematch against Liston the following year. This time, Ali knocked out Liston in the first round. The photo of him standing over Liston is perhaps one of the most famous in sporting history.

Ali has a winner within. He would prove it over and over against the likes of Joe Frazier and George Foreman. He was counted out and proved the critics wrong time after time. Boxing experts thought him too soft. The media thought him too arrogant.

In no fight, however, would Ali demonstrate the winner within more than in his fight with Parkinson's disease. Parkinson's is a devastating disease of the nervous system. In healthy people, nerve cells use a brain chemical called dopamine to help control muscle movement. Parkinson's disease occurs when the nerve cells in the brain that make dopamine are slowly destroyed. Without dopamine, the nerve cells in that part of the brain cannot properly send messages. This leads to the loss of muscle function. The damage gets worse with time. The most obvious symptoms are shaking, rigidity, slowness of movement, and difficulty with walking and gait. While not fatal in itself, research shows that people with Parkinson's are two to five times more likely to have a marked reduction in life expectancy.

According to writer David Remnick, Ali thinks about death all the time now. Ali says, "Do good deeds. Visit hospitals. Judgment Day is coming. Wake up and it's Judgment Day . . . Thinking about after. Thinking about paradise."[3]

Some medical experts say that Ali's boxing contributed to his Parkinson's, but there is no clear evidence to that fact. One thing is certain, however: Ali's boxing *prepared* him for his fight against Parkinson's.

The winner within Ali was built, refined, and bolstered over the years. Whether it was Sonny Liston, Ken Norton, Joe Frazier, or George Foreman, Ali faced the toughest heavyweight fighters in history with courage and amazing, self-generated confidence. In preparation for these brutal bouts, he learned hard work, focus, optimism, and self-discipline. During the bouts he learned to fight alone, without teammates to help, and endured some of the fiercest opponents in history.

Nowadays, Ali still stands in the ring and fights alone. But in hindsight, it's as if God put him in boxing and forced him to fight the mightiest men on earth by himself to prepare him for the decades he would spend fighting what some consider to be the mightiest disease on earth.

INSIGHTS FROM JAKE

I have learned a lot from my experience fighting cancer that has prepared me for a life without sight. I am learning a lot from a life without sight that is preparing me for my next challenge. One of the most important things I have learned is to stay calm and not imagine the worst possible outcome. It's important to focus on the best possible outcome. By doing this you'll have an optimistic view on the situation. You'll also think clearly so you can make better decisions on what to do. The worst possible thing is to panic and make rash decisions, which will bring out more stress or even make the outcome of the situation worse.

Another important thing I've learned is to always remain patient. This doesn't just apply to waiting for lab results or a test grade. This applies to all situations, and most importantly, it applies spiritually. Waiting upon the Lord is extremely helpful and will give you a sense of peace.

The Lord tells us to be patient, because God's time is different from ours. I realize when I pray to the Lord I have to be patient. You should have faith, and pray with conviction and belief, but do not have expectations that the prayer will be answered in your time frame. Prayers are answered in God's time frame. Be patient and never give up hope. To have faith is to know God is there and that he loves us. He has the best plan for us.

In going through adversity, I learned it is necessary to express feelings and to communicate with friends and family. This relieved the stress and also let the people around me know how I was feeling. Family and friends can help you get through problems by showing compassion; this gave me a sense that people cared about me and that they were trying to understand what I was going through.

I have learned that in the most difficult times I can rely on my family, friends, teachers, and church family to comfort and support me. I have been blessed with amazing people in my life who have mentored me, supported me, encouraged me, and sacrificed for me. They have let me be myself and have provided me opportunities to rise above the situation in which I have found myself.

I know there have been many people who have prayed for me and still do. This is a great comfort when I start to feel discouraged. God put us here to help one another. The love I have received from others during my most trying times has taught me that love is the best medicine. I am on a mission to show the same love and encouragement to others that they have shown to me. I have established a foundation, the Out of Sight Faith Foundation, not only to help find cures for cancer, but also to reach out to others in need of help, love, and support.

The Power of Choice: Living Without Procrastination and Fear

Remember as a child dreaming about what you could become in life? Whether it was an astronaut, dancer, or firefighter, the dreams of our youth have all but faded for many of us. What keeps our winner within from shining forth in our life? Why can't we show more discipline to reach our goals? Where is the fire inside and energy to achieve our dreams? For most of us, procrastination and fear get in the way.

Believe it or not, stress plays a more significant role in our lives than we know or imagine. When our stress levels rise, we react. Our nervous systems increase our heart rate and blood pressure, redirecting blood flow to our hearts, muscles, and brains. Our bodies naturally do this to prepare us to respond to danger.

Repeated stress causes our systems to be constantly operating outside their norms, lowering our ability to function normally. When we're overly stressed, we procrastinate or put off doing hard things. We naturally, in our subconscious, put things off to find temporary relief from the feeling and effects of stress. For example, it's not out of the ordinary for a college student who is facing a tough exam to do everything but study for the exam. He'll watch TV, snack, or waste time with friends. All the while, inside, his stress level rises as he engages in an ongoing inner dialogue in which he keeps telling himself he needs to prepare for the exam or he's going to fail. This fear of failure elevates his stress levels. He then finds even more short-term ways to relieve the stress.

When the student snacks on his favorite food, his stress level decreases for a short period of time. He feels better. But when he's done, he knows he's now even further behind, causing his stress level to increase again. So he turns back to the behavior again for short-term relief. This destructive cycle of coping with stress is quite common in our everyday lives. Then the long-term effects of this behavior begin to accumulate. We aren't as healthy, we don't feel happy, we don't perform in our jobs, and we open ourselves up to ongoing negative self-criticism.

The more stressful or painful something is for us, the more likely we are to sabotage ourselves by seeking relief and avoiding the painful task ahead. After we repeat the temporary avoidance over and over again, it becomes habit. We become addicted to the temporary relief. We develop the habit of not doing difficult tasks.

Developing the winner within requires that we learn to do the hard things in life with urgency and without procrastination or fear. When we're in the habit of procrastination, we feel like victims. We feel as if we "have to" do things. When we "have to," we lack motivation and freedom. We feel unable to change our circumstances or exercise the self-discipline necessary to get things done.

> Developing the winner within requires that we learn to do the hard things in life with urgency, and without procrastination or fear.

When we think in terms of "I choose to" rather than "I have to," we experience less stress. With less stress, we avoid the cycle of procrastination. When we avoid procrastinating, we're more successful. Then our self-confidence increases, which helps us do the hard things the next time around. This upward cycle leads us to become better people than we are today.

I learned about the power of choice when my oldest daughter, Kristen, was five years old and learning to ride a bike. It was a sunny Saturday morning, and I decided it was the day for her to master riding her bike without training wheels. I went to the garage, took out my wrench, and promptly removed the training wheels from her bike. I called her outside and proclaimed that she was about to ride a bike without training wheels. I could see in her eyes that she was afraid. It hadn't been her decision. She reluctantly climbed aboard the bike, and I ran alongside her, encouraging her to pedal and take control of the balance of her bike. But she couldn't. She was too afraid of falling to take control. After thirty minutes, we both gave up, discouraged. It had been about what I wanted, not what she wanted. Therefore, it didn't work.

It was only a few days later that one of her friends came to our house. Her friend had mastered riding a bike without training wheels. Of course, Kristen wanted to be like her friend, so she went to the garage, retrieved her bike, and with only a few practice runs and encouragement from her friend, started riding with ease.

Why could she do what she had failed to do only a few days earlier? She rode without fear when she *wanted* to do it. When she *had* to, she was afraid, tentative, and stressed. When she wanted to, she was adventurous, bold, and enthusiastic. It is the same for us in almost any endeavor. When we want to, the adventurous feelings rise up inside us and elevate our creativity. There is unlimited power when we choose.

How do we change a "have to" way of thinking into a "choose to" way of thinking? Let's start with what doesn't work. Threats don't work. Punishments don't work. If we physically exercise because we are afraid of gaining weight, we may still exercise. It worked, right? Wrong. Fear may cause us to do a task in the short term, but we still feel stress, pressure, and resentment. Using threats as our means for motivation is like pushing a rope. The more we push, the more it bends when being pushed. Pulling a rope, however, is an entirely different story. When being pulled, ropes don't bend under pressure. We're much the same way.

Dr. Neil Fiore says, "It is not the discipline, willpower, or pressure from others that facilitates adherence to a challenging course of action. Rather, it is the freedom to choose among alternatives, the personal commitment to a mission, and the willingness to take responsibility for the consequences of our decisions that steels the will and emboldens the spirit."[4]

INSIGHTS FROM JAKE

In the last several months my golf swing had really been taking shape. Lesson after lesson had been paying off, and I could really feel my ball-striking ability improve. It showed up in my iron play, where the ball just seemed to rocket off the club. It is a great feeling. But I was continuing to struggle with my chip shots around the green. So I decided to put some real focus on going out to practice around the green on three specific days a week over a couple of months. It was around February that I made this plan, and the weather was not cooperating real well despite being in Southern California. We were going through one of the wettest winters on record, which made practicing pretty tough.

One late Friday afternoon the rain was coming down in buckets. I can always tell the difference between light rain and a real rain in the way it sounds when it hits my house. This particular rain was off the charts. When I spoke to my dad on his way home from work, he mentioned it was raining pretty hard on the roadways, almost hoping I would tell him I wasn't up for practice that day.

"Yep, it's raining hard here too," I told him.

My dad told me he would be home in about twenty minutes. And then he asked again, perhaps with one final gasp of hope, if I still planned to go practice my chip shots in the downpour.

"Yep, we're going," I said.

"Okay," he replied. It was probably the most unexcited "okay" I had ever heard out of my dad.

When he got home, we threw on some weather gear and headed out to the course. No one was there when we arrived, and on the way to the practice green we were stepping in puddles and rivers of fallen rain everywhere. We were soaked in a matter of seconds. It was this type of practice that would sharpen not only my golfing skills, but also my golfing character. Neither of us really wanted to do this, but we did. It was a set plan, and we followed through with it despite the rain. I followed my plan rather than my mood. I practiced in the pouring rain for a good two hours, and we were as wet as we could possibly get when it was over.

It's funny that I don't remember many of my practice days in the sun, but I will remember that practice day for a long time. It seems we are shaped more by the difficult things we do.

Game Plan for the Winner Within

To develop the winner within, we all need a game plan. But it's important to follow the right principles in planning. Here they are:

Choose your course of action.

When we are free to choose a course of action, we are motivated because it's something we want. The problem is, sometimes we think we aren't free to choose. For example, you might feel stuck in a job that isn't fulfilling; you feel that you can't choose another career because you're not trained to do anything else. But if you are headed on a course that isn't what you would choose, you can set up the next five years as time to transition to a new career.

Dr. Michael Kroth teaches the principle of planning your career in five-year segments. In five years, you can get a degree, learn a new skill, network with new people, and make a significant change. Kroth was fifty when he chose to return to school for his PhD. It took him five years. He went to school and worked extra hours to provide for his family. He says it didn't feel like extra work because he had a clear goal in mind.

Today Dr. Kroth teaches at a major university and is living the career he chose. The point is that when we limit our thinking to the short term, we can't choose. We feel trapped. But when we expand our thinking to a longer period, like five years, we gain the time and means to realistically choose to make a change.

Know where you're headed and clearly define the outcome.

Clarity trumps persuasion. The more immediate and clear the goal and reward, the more likely you are to be motivated to do what it takes to earn the reward. For example, if you need to lose weight, set a clear goal to lose twenty pounds. Don't set a goal to "diet better." That may be the right thing to do, but it isn't the end outcome, nor is it clear. Clearly defining the end outcome gives you a vision of what you'd look like if you lost twenty pounds. Visualize yourself thinner. That creates the magnetic pull of motivation.

Oddly enough, sometimes we sabotage ourselves. We set a vague end goal because it leaves room for ambiguity and failure. For example, if our goal is simply to lose some weight, then we can achieve that goal if we lose one, two, or three pounds. The vagueness of the goal robs us of the power of visualizing ourselves having achieved the end goal. If our goal is to lose twenty pounds, there is a clear and defined end objective. It's that objective that allows us to visualize our end goal clearly and that creates motivation.

Author Brian Tracy says, "Successful people have very clear goals. They know who they are and what they want. They write them down and make plans for their accomplishment."[5] When we set realistic and very clear goals, it increases our faith in its plausibility, defines it so we know exactly what to do, and clarifies so that progress can be measured and rewarded. Periodic progress is key to the self-confidence necessary to achieve goals.

Direct your energy toward your end goal.

If we spend our energy making excuses or avoiding the hard things, we lose our motivation. Have you ever set a goal to get up earlier in the morning to exercise? On the first day when the alarm goes off, you sit up in bed and engage in a dialogue with Self #1 and Self #2. Self #1 is the side of you that is motivated to reach a goal. Self #2 is the procrastinator. The dialogue goes something like this:

SELF #1: "You need to get up and get going."

SELF #2: "Yeah, but you could sleep in and exercise this afternoon."

SELF #1: "You won't. You're too tired in the afternoon. Get up."

SELF #2: "Lie down for a just a few more minutes . . ."

This dialogue goes on and on. In fact, if you immediately get up and get moving, you could be at the gym before your inner dialogue has run its course. How do you find the motivation to get up and moving? Put your energy and thought toward the end goal.

When we direct our energy toward the end goal, it gives us energy to think creatively about how to reach it. When we engage the creative parts of our brains, we awaken the adventurous spirit. The winner within is born of adventure. With an adventurous spirit, we avoid the fear of being overwhelmed.

> Put your energy and thought toward the end goal.

One thing that keeps us from exercising our adventurous spirit can be the reluctance to leave what is familiar and easy. This can keep us from stepping out into the unknown. Don't buy into that natural way of thinking. Our bodies and minds are designed to keep us safe, to repeat over and over again what is most comfortable. This is nature's way of helping us survive. You won't *feel* like stepping out of your comfort zone, but you have to recognize it and step anyway. Action always precedes feeling.

If you've ever trained for a marathon, you know about forcing your body to step out of its comfort zone. In fact, running 26.2 miles feels impossible. But by keeping to your training schedule week after week, you stretch yourself a little farther with each long run.

When you follow a precise training program that forces you to push beyond what your body would naturally allow you to do, you soon discover that you can go farther and faster than you ever thought possible. Then the adventurous part of your work kicks in as you step up your workouts to include sprints and cross training. These variations give added energy to your plan without changing the end goal. Finally, the marathon day arrives. The winner within can carry you through because you've pushed beyond your perceived limits so many times in your training that one more time is simple.

Take personal responsibility.

"Take responsibility not just for your successes, but for your failures as well," President Obama told graduates at Kalamazoo High School. "The truth is, no matter how hard you work, you won't necessarily ace every class or succeed in every job. There will be times when you screw up . . . And when that happens, it's the easiest thing in the world to start looking around for someone to blame. Your professor was too hard, your boss was a jerk, the coach was playing favorites, your friend just didn't understand."[6]

Don't make excuses.

INSIGHTS FROM JAKE

Golf is full of so many opportunities to mess up. There are a lot of ways a golf swing can come off track or go wrong. When you add to that the fact that I can't see the golf ball or my swing, it gets even more challenging.

In the past year I have been challenged with learning a new golf swing, in part because I lost my sight, but also because I grew more than a foot in height! These are two unbelievable physical changes that could wreak havoc on any athlete in any sport. So I've had to really learn the keys to a good swing.

For a typical golfer, before the swing even starts, he can make a mistake. He can be set up wrong with his feet out of place, the club not set at the proper angle, the back and head too far forward or too far back, or the weight on the feet distributed improperly. Imagine doing that with no sight at all!

If you get all that stuff right, you can then begin to take the club back and start the swing. Bringing the club back is a challenge in and of itself. The club can't start too far inside or outside. Then the distance the club is brought back is important; you don't want to overswing or underswing. The club should always stay on the right swing plane. Any club that comes off its swing plane will automatically cost a golfer at some point during impact.

Then comes the transition at the top of the back swing. Every golf teacher in the world will tell you this transition is as important as it gets. Transition means the point at which the club changes direction from going back to coming forward. These same golf teachers will tell you that this is the point where most golfers mess up. They just can't get the transition right. Then comes pace and rhythm. You need to have the proper pace coming back down. The speed of the club is important; the faster the better, but you need to stay within yourself, whatever that means.

I could go on with other swing concepts, such as avoiding the reverse pivot, staying square at impact, the importance of the fraction of a second right before impact (another biggie), staying behind the ball, follow-through, patience, and finally balance. It's a lot. And any one of them can go wrong. When one does, it generally means a bad shot.

But what I have learned is that these challenges are only opportunities to make my swing better. When I had to learn how to swing a club blind, I started to really learn how to swing. My growth and blindness gave me the chance to really learn the game and become a better golfer. It has not been easy. I hit a lot of bad shots. Sometimes I completely miss the ball on my swing. It makes me question my ability and confuses my focus. But I've stayed focused on the end goal.

I have also stayed focused on being coachable. Being blind has made me a lot more coachable. What a great thing to learn! I have stayed square in my stance, and moved the club back as told, and transitioned as told, and felt my rhythm and tempo, and felt my hand position, and remained balanced and athletic in my finish.

I've come to learn that without challenges in golf, the game would lose its essence. Most importantly, I've learned that without life's challenges, life would lose its meaning.

We can supplement our game plan with three more steps: choose when we are going to live, find the right solution, and know what is required.

Choose when you're going to live.

We can't choose when we were born; how can we choose when we live? The truth is, we do it every day. Many of us live our lives in the past. We constantly use the past as an excuse. We long for a relationship like we had in the past or a situation that was good but didn't last. We reflect on past days as times when things were better. We use past accomplishments to define who we are today. God made us to look forward, not backward. Who we will become is more important than who we've been. When we choose to live in the past, we automatically forfeit the future. If it seems you can't escape the past, then stop choosing to live there.

While some of us are living in the past, others are living solely in the present, obsessed with the busyness of our lives. It's easy to fill our lives with so many things to do that there isn't time to reflect on who we're becoming. We use our schedules or present circumstances as the reason to put off reconciling a broken friendship or developing a meaningful relationship that may take time and effort. Some of us don't want to think about the past or the future. Both seem equally painful. But there is little satisfaction in the present. As such, the future passes us by every day.

You can choose to live in the future. You can define your future. Waiting for you in the future are times when you'll be greater than yourself—when, through your defining moments, you'll influence others to be better. When you live in the future, you become an agent of hope. You're full of faith. When you look to the future, you don't ignore the present, but you look to make your life and the lives of others happier tomorrow.

Look for the right solution.

Sometimes reaching our goals requires that we do something out of the ordinary. Not necessarily something big, but something different from what we might typically think to do.

In fact, we often overreact and think we need a big change when, in fact, small yet uncomfortable adjustments would get the job done just fine. For example, after receiving some critical feedback at work, you might overreact and think you need to find a new job, when small improvements in your work performance would more than suffice. Often we must be prepared to act in a way we might not otherwise act.

You may have heard the story of the Weibertreu Castle in Germany. In 1140, the castle and its occupants, including the Duke of Welf, were under siege from the Duke of Swabia and his brother King Konrad III. Konrad and his men were fearless, skilled, and ruthless. The siege was long, but finally Konrad conquered the defenses of the castle and was about to lay everything to waste. The Duke of Welf was obliged at last to offer his surrender, and Konrad granted him permission to depart in safety.

But the Duke's wife, the Lady Uta, did not trust this fair offer. She knew that Konrad hated her husband and would kill all the men as soon as they took possession of the castle. So she sent a message to Konrad to entreat him to grant safe conduct to her and all the other women in the garrison, and that they might come out with as many of their valuables as they could carry on their backs. The letter read: "We, the women of the castle, humbly realize that our fate is in your hands. We ask only that you allow us to leave at sunrise tomorrow with our children and whatever we can carry on our backs. For this we entreat you and submit our lives to your mercy."

This request was freely granted. The next morning at sunrise, when the castle gates were opened, out stepped the women with their children following behind. The women were not carrying their gold or valuables, but their own husbands on their backs. On the backs of unmarried women were their own brothers or fathers. Each woman staggered under the weight of her burden. It is said Konrad was affected to the point of tears by this extraordinary display and remained true to his word and let the men live. Hence the castle was named Weibertreu, or Castle of the Loyal Wives.

Know what is required.

What is required to live up to your goal? In 1 Samuel, the armies of Israel had been camped opposite the Philistines for forty days. Each day, Goliath presented himself and verbally challenged and ridiculed the Israelite army. Among the soldiers was Eliab, the oldest son of Jesse. Eliab and his two brothers, Abinadab and Shammah, had joined the army to fight. Eliab was the oldest. He had the birthright to stand up at this defining moment. It was his to claim. But fear, not only fear of Goliath, but fear of what others would think of him, kept him from stepping forward.

When Eliab's younger brother David came to camp to bring food to his older brothers, he heard Goliath scream his insults to Israel and issue a challenge to any man who dared face him. David began to chastise the men around him. "Who is this uncircumcised Philistine, that he should defy the armies of the living God?" (1 Sam. 17:26).

But Eliab scolded David. He was embarrassed that his younger brother was so bold as to speak up in front of the soldiers. He was afraid of what people would think. But David, undeterred at this defining moment, exercised his faith, persuaded the king to let him fight, and defeated Goliath. In so doing, David seized his future and defined the future of his family.

Eliab didn't live up to what was, by all rights, his defining moment. He was the oldest and in the position to do what David did. Yet he would not. He was afraid. When we know what God expects, we act with certainty. We aren't afraid. We don't care what others think. We take appropriate risks. We step out of our comfort zones. When we exercise our faith, sometimes we do things we might not otherwise think we can do. But through these experiences, we broaden our experience, lift our lives, and help those around us.

So find the winner within. Procrastinate less. Act more. Look for your defining moment.

Courage to Never Give Up

Hundreds of books have been written about the courage possessed by mountain climbers, test pilots, and explorers. Not many books, however, are written about the courage of professional bass fisherman. Bass fishing doesn't require courage, right? Well, when it comes to one bass fisherman in particular, nothing could be further from the truth.

Clay Dyer was born on May 23, 1978, without any lower limbs, no arm on the left side and a partial arm on the right. Clay started fishing at age five and began tournament fishing at fifteen. You may ask, "How can he fish with only one partial arm and no hands?" Clay uses his chin to hold the fishing rod against his neck and turns the reel with his partial arm. He ties the lures to his fishing line with his mouth and tongue. He retrieves his lure from the mouth of fish in the same way.

Clay has fished in more than two hundred bass tournaments and placed first in about twenty state tournaments. He attracted the attention of several high-level sponsors, but after six years, he was disqualified from professional competition because of a rule requiring that all participants be able to render aid to others in the case of an accident. But Clay was undeterred. He worked with the organizations to allow him to fish. In 2006, at the age of twenty-eight, he qualified for the FLW series, the apex of bass tournaments.

Despite his excellent skills, Clay has yet to make the final cut in a professional tournament. This, however, has not deterred his passion for professional fishing. He refuses to quit. He says, "When I was about [four and a half] years old or so, I said, 'Daddy, why did God make me like this?' My dad looked at me and said, 'Son, I don't know, but I know God doesn't make mistakes.' When I look back on it, I realize that I didn't see it at the time, but God knew when He made me, He made me for a purpose to be able to go out and witness and encourage people to live for Him."[7]

Why do some people seem to naturally have a no-matter-what mind-set and others don't? Do people naturally have the winner within, or is it developed? The truth is that a no-matter-what attitude isn't free. It comes at a price. Disappointments and other challenges in life are the price we pay to acquire a no-matter-what mind-set.

Would Tom Brady be the MVP quarterback he is today if he'd been drafted in the first round rather than the sixth? Would Itzhak Perlman be the talented concert violinist he is if he had not contracted polio and lost the use of his legs? Would Lucille Ball have been as driven to become an award-winning actress and comedienne if she hadn't been told by the head instructor of the John Murray Anderson Drama School to "try another profession"?

When God sends obstacles our way, he also sends the opportunities for us to increase our resolve. He turns our focus from the bumps in the road, which would typically deter us, to the road itself because we learn how to navigate the bumps. Once we traverse an obstacle, we can see ourselves overcoming the remaining obstacles.

Ever wonder why a golf ball has dents or dimples? Wouldn't a golf ball be better as a smooth, round ball? The truth is that a golf ball that has flaws flies farther. The dimples on a golf ball create turbulence, or more accurately, turbulent flow. As a perfectly smooth sphere travels through the air, it pushes the air to either side. Because there is no drag on the surface of the ball, there is no "pull" to keep the airflow tucked in tightly around the ball. So, the air is pushed outward, creating a larger wake on either side of the ball.

When a golf ball has dimples, it creates a slight drag or pull toward the surface of the ball and a turbulent wake behind the ball. This pulls the air closer in toward the surface of the golf ball, pulling the air along the side and behind the ball. Because the wake is tucked in around the ball, the ball pushes less air as it travels, and therefore flies farther. Interestingly enough, the flaws or dimples on the ball also allow the ball to generate lift as it spins.

Ironically, when you look at a smooth sphere, you would assume it would fly farther. When you see a dimpled golf ball, you assume the dimples would limit the distance the ball could fly. The same thing is true in our lives. When we first look at obstacles or mistakes, we see them as limiting. But what we soon learn is that the knowledge we gain from our flaws and mistakes actually allows us to steer our lives more effectively and soar to new heights.

What Is Your Defining Moment?

Suzanne Hobbs and her husband had tried for years to have a child. Yet God hadn't blessed them with children. They had visited doctors, been tested, and tried every available treatment, but they could not have children. They applied for adoption, but no children were available for adoption. Suzanne wanted to be a mother. She wondered why God would not bless her with a child. Why had God taken away her chance, despite her prayers and faith?

Suzanne worked as a reporter and news anchor in Idaho Falls, Idaho. Over her fourteen-year career, she had covered most of the major crime stories and had established relationships with police officers in the area. One morning in October 2000, she received a call from a police officer, giving her a tip that a man who had been digging through a dumpster, looking for aluminum cans, had discovered the dead body of an abandoned baby.

Suzanne hurried to the crime scene. She watched as the detectives climbed into the dumpster and began their investigation. As she watched, she was despondent and angry.

What a waste, she thought. *What I would have given to have that child. How could something like this happen?*

She watched with tears in her eyes as the detectives lifted the tiny body from the dumpster to the van and drove away. She stated in her news report later that day that police soon located the teenage girl who had hidden her pregnancy from her family and delivered the baby in her bathtub before abandoning it in the alley.

Suzanne later interviewed the father of the teenage mother. He told Suzanne that he had learned about a Safe Haven Law in other states. The law allows mothers to leave children at designated safe havens, like hospitals or fire stations, without the fear of prosecution. He felt that if that law had been in place, his daughter would not have abandoned her baby in a dumpster, and the baby would be alive today.

"I knew, right then," Suzanne said, "I had a mission and it was personal."

Suzanne went to work. She contacted her state senator and began to lobby for a Safe Haven Act for Idaho. She wrote letters, made phone calls, and brought the issue to light. Because of her determination and hard work, the law was passed the following year. At the signing of the bill into law, Suzanne was covering the story. When the governor signed the bill, he called Suzanne to the front of the room to recognize her. He gave her the pen used to sign the bill into law. But the story doesn't end there.

Suzanne and her husband continued to try to become pregnant, with no success. They waited, without success, for a baby to adopt. One day, Suzanne was talking to her sister and told her she felt something was going to happen soon, that God had a plan for a baby to come into her life. Then, one morning in July, the phone rang and a caseworker for the Department of Welfare told her about an abandoned baby who was left at the hospital the previous day. She told Suzanne that her name was chosen from the list of potential parents who were trying to adopt. If they wanted the baby girl, they could adopt her.

So the necessary paperwork was completed and Lilly found her new home with Suzanne and her husband. Lilly was Idaho's fifth Safe Haven baby. Since then, more than twenty abandoned babies have been legally and safely adopted because of the Safe Haven Act in Idaho.

If Suzanne had been given children earlier, she might not have been as apt to follow her instinct and pursue the Safe Haven Act in Idaho. She would likely not have Lilly as part of her life. The truth is, God has a plan.

Like Suzanne, we all have defining moments that can easily pass us by. But if we're watching and listening to the winners within, we can seize the moment and change our futures. These defining moments often come to us as fleeting thoughts; I believe these thoughts to be inspired. I have learned to treat every good thought as inspiration. When you do, you soon learn whether it came from God, and you never miss a defining moment. No doubt, we've let that inspiration come and go hundreds of times in our lives. But what if we started living and not let one more pass us by?

Winners seize the moment. They don't let the times define them. They don't let situations or circumstances dictate their direction. They define their time. They define their circumstances. They put their imprints, their stamps, on the world. They treat most moments as defining moments.

To seize our defining moments, we must realize God has put us here for a purpose. We can live with our eyes open, looking for our defining moments and being willing to act. Who knows if, like Suzanne's, the initiative you take today will come back years hence to bless your life significantly?

In Summary

- Look for the winner within. God has uniquely prepared you for your future.
- Recognize that procrastination and fear can keep us from those things we were meant to do.
- Choose your course of action, know where you're headed, and direct your energy toward that goal.
- Live in the future, not the past. Be prepared for what comes your way.
- Look for the defining moments in your life.

6

OUR TRUE POTENTIAL

We don't see things as they are, we see them as we are.

—ANAÏS NIN

You may have heard the story about a man who was the mayor of his town. He was invited to be the grand marshal of the town's local parade. He and his wife were riding down Main Street at the head of the parade in a vintage convertible. While they were waving at the various people in the crowd, the mayor spotted his wife's former boyfriend, who owned the local gas station. He chuckled and said to his wife, "Aren't you glad you didn't marry him? If you had, you'd be working at a gas station." To which she replied, "No. If I had married him, he would be the mayor!"

The choices we make determine who we become. Who we marry, the professions we choose, and the friends we associate with all play key roles in our development in life. We make dozens of choices each day; most of them we think are small and without significance. Yet these choices often have lasting consequences, and unfortunately some of our choices are poor.

Why do we make poor choices? There are a lot of reasons. Sometimes, we lack experience, perspective, or maturity. We all want to have better judgment and greater maturity, but where do we get it? There's not a school for maturity. Research in child development is replete with techniques to help children develop and grow. There are clear stages of child development and established steps for helping a child gain greater understanding and maturity. But it seems that when we reach the age of eighteen, the literature stops. It's as if we're supposed to be fully developed adults on the day we become legal adults. Of course, this does not reflect reality.

The Stages of Adult Development

What most people don't know is that there are clear stages of adult development. These stages of development follow one's increasing ability to cope, interact effectively with others, deal with life's challenges with perspective, and structure experience in a way that makes sense. By understanding these stages of growth and where we stand in our own development, we can exercise better judgment, make better choices, and live more happily.

Researchers have shown that our development follows an expanding spiral, not a straight vertical line. As we progress upward in our development, we not only rise, but also broaden and expand our thinking. As we grow, our ever-expanding circle of influence and perspective allows us to navigate relationships and think in a broader, more complex way.

There are three dimensions to our development and growth. The first is behavioral, or how we interact, cope, and master our lives. The second is emotional, or how we feel about things, perceive experiences, and put up defenses. The third is intellectual, or how we think, make meaning of experiences, and interpret things in our lives. To move forward in life, we must consider the behavioral, emotional, and intellectual dimensions at each stage of our development.

Jane Loevinger, a respected researcher in psychology and development, created the Washington University Sentence Completion Test (SCT). This test asks participants to finish incomplete sentences and uses their responses to determine where they fit within the eight stages of development, each stage representing a larger, more complex and integrated way of seeing and acting in the world. This test has been widely administered to a large number and variety of adults.

Let's briefly review these stages from the STC test, looking at the percentage of adults living at each stage, and describing their characteristics. As you read about each stage, ask yourself, "What stage best describes me, and what might be keeping me from moving beyond my current way of behaving or thinking?" Not only is there great value in understanding where we are in our own development, but also where others are in theirs. If we really want to understand another person, we need to know where they are in their own evolution.

Stage 1: Impulsive

Though most of the people in this stage are children, 4.3 percent of the adult population still falls into this development level. At this stage in our development, we are governed mostly by our impulses. The way we interact with others and the world seems random and retaliatory. If good things happen to us, we're happy. At this stage, we're polarized in our thinking: things are good or bad, people are nice or mean. There is no middle ground. This polarization extends to how we think about ourselves. We either have to be perfect or we feel like total failures.

We're immature in our ability to talk about our feelings, and unable to step apart from our behavior to assess how we think or feel about it. We take comfort in repetitiveness and routine. We stay where things are safe and our needs are met. At this stage, we may be easily confused, anxious, and overwhelmed.

Stage 2: Self-Protective

At this stage of development, adults often have two sides: the inner self (how they really feel) and the outer self (what they want the world to see). If we're at this stage, we maintain a false outer shell in order to protect ourselves. About 11.1 percent of the adult population operates at this developmental level.

At this level, we're fearful we'll get into trouble, something bad will happen, or we'll be embarrassed. In order to protect ourselves, we look out for trouble and avoid it. It's a "me against the world" way of thinking. We relate to almost everyone with a low level of trust.

As a result of the protective nature and immature social skills, we don't understand relationships that aren't based on force or power. We often use force to get our way. We explode easily and blame others for our shortcomings. We feel threatened in our interactions. Showing weakness of any kind is dangerous. We think, *The more others know about me, the more they can take advantage of me.*

Others perceive self-protective adults as being bullheaded. But the truth is they are compensating for their insecurities. Self-protective adults are often obsessed with their appearances and tend to determine their value compared to others based on the way they look. Controlling the way they look and appear is easier than interacting with others and risking being valued on what they think or feel.

Stage 3: Conformist

Adults in this stage create their self-identity by their participation within a group. The group is often a family, team, or a group of people with the same superficial similarities. Being part of a larger entity allows them to be protected personally, yet participate in the power of the group. They want to be part of a group so badly they will conform to the perceived rules of the group, political party, or profession in order to be accepted. For example, adults in this stage might adopt labels like "yuppie" or "hippie." They conform to avoid detection. They find their self-worth in membership. About 15.5 percent of adults are in the conformist stage.

Conformists may try to keep up with the Joneses by buying new clothes, cars, or houses in order to have the status symbols necessary to give the impression of success. They believe having a pleasing personality is important to fit in socially. They care about what others think and seek the prestige found in group association. They are often neat in appearance and define themselves by the expectations of the group or image to which they subscribe.

Conformists often can't determine appropriate boundaries in relationships. They can be codependent. They interact with others based on whether they fit into the same group. They avoid deep feelings and motives because this risks their association. They are concerned with social acceptance and group norms.

Not all conformists put on the appearance of success. They put on whatever image allows them to participate in the group. They overly exaggerate the positive effect of the group to bolster their own self-image.

Stage 4: Expert

At this stage, in order to be valued, adults not only need to be accepted (like conformists), but must also be better than others. They often have high moral standards and a sense of superiority. They find value in ridicule. They enjoy oppositional battles with others who defend different positions. They can be argumentative and opinionated. Approximately one in four (26.5%) of adults are included in this group.

In the expert stage, adults are able to mentally and emotionally step apart from themselves or their way of thinking to reflect on their behavior from a distance. They can think about their way of being. They can be introspective. Possessing this newfound introspection, they are often full of solutions for every problem.

Experts fear losing their sense of superiority or uniqueness. Because they are aware of their own separate personhood and value it, they fear getting reabsorbed back into a common group of people. They are rarely at a loss for an answer, but are not available for inspection or scrutiny themselves. Being in charge is a chief trait.

Stage 5: Achiever

Adults in this stage can belong to several diverse groups at the same time. They no longer rely solely on expertise for self-validation. They have chosen, based on analysis, goals they would like to achieve. They are about accomplishing. They are idealistic and often in love with the theoretical. They join groups or associate with others based on whether those groups or associations can help them reach their goals.

They can navigate across differing opinions without feeling torn about competing loyalties. They are interested in causes and uncovering the truth about things. They are willing to work toward improving the world. They are motivated, in part, by guilt. They believe it's important to live up to what they have chosen to believe in.

Achievers can be highly self-critical; they will apologize if it helps them move on and continue in their productiveness. They are aware of their weaknesses and strengths, and able to revise their actions to accomplish a goal. They fear being conformists, but they like things to be predictable and get frustrated when they are not. They want more knowledge, and often step away from their way of behaving in the world to assess its effectiveness. About 23.6 percent of the adult population is living at this stage of development.

Stage 6: Individualist

At this stage, adults begin to realize that the things important to them at the earlier stages (appearance, comparing themselves to others, and achievement) are no longer important. They are comfortable as individuals and may withdraw to some degree from external affairs to turn inward, help others, or pursue their own paths.

About 11.1 percent of adults are individualists. Instead of pursuing the future, they want to live in the moment and pay attention to feelings. They can be more interested in the process than the outcome. They want to find out who they really are. It's easy to think that individualists are going through midlife crises because they reevaluate their lives and question their authenticity.

Individualists can seem depressed because they become isolated in their sense of self. However, they are also skilled at interaction, spontaneity, and living life free from restrictions. They are constantly seeking a new truth about themselves.

Stage 7: Strategist

Adults at this stage have moved beyond looking inward and finding who they really are. They strive to make meaning and tell a new story in life. Strategists are creating meaningful lives for themselves and others. They will often use stories to create insight, and possess very high self-esteem. They have become much less cynical than they once were. Strategists represent about 4.9 percent of the adult population.

They are now capable of reaching back into their pasts and accepting the parts of their lives that were not good, even events or periods of time that they have previously put aside. They accept who they have been and who they are today. They feel responsible for leaving a legacy. They can handle distressing emotions with maturity and are tolerant with others.

Strategists fear unfulfilled potential. They want to help others grow and develop. While wanting to help, they trust that others have the capacity to make meaning of their poor choices and will change their lives. In relationships, they desire some autonomy. They are able to use mature defenses, such as humor, altruism, or anticipation. Most often they are charismatic individuals who can express themselves with ease and are comfortable with other people.

Stage 8: Alchemist

An alchemist is someone who makes something that is common uncommon. Adults at the alchemist stage are able to see the ways we make meaning and construct realities. They are very aware of how they think and feel. They are not deceived by previous ways of making meaning and are capable of a broader view of experience. Less than 2 percent of the population ever reaches this level of development.

Adults at this stage think beyond their own lifetime. They accept and easily deal with tension and weaknesses. Given their experience, they're able to appreciate the purpose of trials, consequences, and social interaction in helping human beings to develop and grow. They can have productive relationships with people regardless of their station in life, gender, personality, or age.

At this stage, adults are more inclined to intuition and rational deliberation. They can go about pursuing their purpose in life with full realization of their fears. They are aware of their false feelings and perceptions. Alchemists are exceptionally good mentors. They help others reframe their experiences and find courage. Most of all they can see clearly how meaning is constructed, and this allows them to help others make meaning in a transformative way.

INSIGHTS FROM JAKE

A few days after I learned I would be losing my sight, many thoughts rushed through my mind. *Will I be able to attend my junior high school? Will my friends still treat me the same way? Will I be able to play sports? Will I be able to continue my passion for golf?* The first weekend following the news from my doctor, my dad and I went to play a round of golf at one of our favorite courses in Palm Desert, California. It's a place we often go to get away from it all and just play golf. On this occasion, it was more about the getting away and less about the golf.

On the drive out, I asked my dad if there were any really special courses in the desert—like a top-one-hundred course. About four years ago, my dad received an insert in a golf magazine that named the top one hundred public golf courses in the United States. We reviewed the list and found that we had already played one or two of them. We decided right then to make it a mission to play all one hundred courses. I had my dad call back home on his cell phone to see if Mom could grab the insert and review it for any Palm Desert area courses. Sure enough, she found one in La Quinta, a small community right next to Palm Desert. My dad immediately called the course and made a tee time and we drove straight there.

It was a hot October day in the desert, with little relief from the one-hundred-plus-degree temperature, but I was just happy to be able to tee it up. More so, I was happy to be in the desert with my dad. It started out as a typical round of golf. We were hitting some good shots, rolling in a few putts, and just enjoying the day. At some point on the back nine, I asked my dad to help me with something. I told him I wanted to start swinging the club with my eyes closed. It had been bugging me all day, actually since the moment I heard I would lose my physical sight. As much as I wanted to continue playing golf, I guess there was some form of question in my mind as to whether it would really be possible.

So after a particular tee shot, I had him grab me from the golf cart and lead me to my ball as though I was blind. I kept my eyes closed the whole time. My dad explained the layout, gave me the yardage, selected an 8-iron, and then he lined me up. It felt a little weird, standing over the ball and not seeing it, but I took my normal swing. I connected and then waited for a sound. I could hear it off to the right. It couldn't have been a great 8-iron because it sounded too close. Yet I could visualize the shot. I tried a few more, and after three or four of them, I finally put one on the green. It wasn't easy, but from that moment on I knew I could do it.

When we got to the green, I wanted to do the same thing on the putting surface. I had my dad walk me onto the green with my eyes closed. Interestingly, I could detect many things with the bottom of my feet as we approached the green. I could tell the transition from the rough to the fringe, and then from the fringe to the putting surface. I could also tell we were walking flat for a while, and then it felt like a gradual incline. My dad confirmed the incline. We paced the steps from my ball to the hole. I could slightly intuit the break. The distance was about fifteen feet.

I have later learned that your feet are ten times more sensitive, and accurate, than your eyes in understanding the undulations of greens or putting surfaces. The feet can feel the breaks without being tricked by lines, coloring, or other visual distractions. The eyes can prove to be very unreliable in reading putts; you would just never suspect that. My dad lined me up and then went to tend the pin. I had him rattle it so I could pick up the distance from sound. I made a nice stroke and put it about three feet past the hole. My dad led me to the second putt and lined me up again.

Now, any golfer can tell you that the sound of a ball dropping into a golf hole has a unique sound like no other. This is one of the more special sounds in the entire universe. It just has a vibrating rattle to it that is like no other. It doesn't matter which course it is; it all sounds the same. Seeing a putt fall in is okay, but hearing the sound is the best! So imagine when I heard this first putt without sight as it hit the bottom of the hole and rattle around for a half second. It was awesome!

It was reassuring that there was so much to this game that I could hold on to. I could make it my own. I could go on knowing I could create tens of thousands of identical sounds. I recognized I would be losing an important aspect of the game, but I wasn't losing everything. At the same time I was gaining a few things. It was immediately clear to me that I would now have to focus less on sight and more on feel, instinct, and sound when putting. I would now have to rely on feel, balance, tempo, and trust when swinging. It was an exciting moment for me, because I knew I could do it. We finished the round, some shots with sight, others without.

I knew continuing my golf game without physical sight wouldn't be without its challenges, because the game of golf is not easy. But within a single afternoon I learned I could play it without physical sight, and I knew

I could play it well. I told my dad after that round that I was not going to give up my dream of playing competitive golf. If anything, it had just been solidified.

Progressing to the Next Stage

After learning about the stages of adult development, you might be asking yourself the question, "How do I move from one stage to the next?" The answer gets at the root of human development. It unlocks the secret to progressing into a happy and mature adult, and it lies in three important steps.

1. Step back and assess your situation.

Harvard professor and psychologist Robert Kegan said, "Something cannot be internalized until we emerge from our embedded-ness in it. . . . When a child is able to have his reflexes rather than be them, he stops thinking he causes the world to go dark each time he closes his eyes."[1]

Consider the working mom who's stuck in the conformist stage. Given her way of thinking, she thinks her happiness depends on being seen as a successful woman. Not only is her house clean and neat, but her children must also live up to the image she sees for herself. If she is embedded in the need to be seen as successful, she may be unable to see that her kids only feel love from her when they are conforming to her image of a successful family. She may be unable to control her temper when her kids don't want to dress or behave in a particular way.

If this mother were able to think objectively about what causes her fear and motivation, she might be able to move beyond it. Stepping back from her embedded-ness would be like seeing her life as a camera would view it. However, when she is faced with the reality of needing to change, she may be afraid to give up her successful appearance. This can be very scary. Many adults won't change and develop to the next level because of the fear of losing what they're used to in life. That's why faith is so uncommon yet so critical to our development in life.

Why is it difficult, if not impossible, for us to let go of our past? We've been living with our perceptions and building our way of making meaning around that way of viewing the world for so long that we can't trust in another view. We are afraid to abandon our way of thinking.

When Jake Olson's way of seeing the world was about to change, he was sad, scared, and discouraged. But he started to anticipate who he could become. He began to think about the new possibilities available to him with his new way of seeing.

2. Get help to see what you can't.

How do you break free from your way of viewing the world if you are stuck in your mind-set? There are two powerful tools to make this happen.

The first is a mentor. A mentor may be a parent, spouse, pastor, friend, or counselor. A mentor who is trustworthy and more advanced in his or her own development can often help you see what you can't see on your own. They can point out the ways in which you perceive things that may not be seeing things as they really are.

> **Reading is to our perspective what exercise is to our body.**

Why a *trusted* mentor? If we trust in their capability and their character, we are able to put faith in what they say. It's that faith that causes us to abandon old ways of thinking and try on the new. We will discuss mentors and mentoring in detail in chapter 7.

The second tool for breaking free from your mind-set is a diet of uplifting words. Through positive messages, we can see new ways of living and thinking. Some people read scriptures daily, others listen to motivational messages, and others are continually reading to improve themselves. Words of inspiration can lift us from one stage of development to the next. Reading is to our perspective what exercise is to our bodies. As Henry Ward Beecher said, "A book is a garden, an orchard, a storehouse, a party, a company by the way, a counselor, a multitude of counselors."[2]

Even as a teenager, Jake gathers wisdom and faith from what he reads. Through his trials and challenges since he lost his sight, he has relied on his family and inspiration from reading to elevate his view of what he can become.

"I love to read God's Word," says Jake. "I think it is amazing that he loves us so much that he left us with a book that guides us and reminds us of that love. Reading and memorizing Scripture has helped me get through my most difficult times. Everyone goes through hard times, and they need to know that there is help and peace and comfort to be found. My favorite verse is Jeremiah 29:11: "'For I know the plans I have for you,' declares the LORD, 'plans to prosper you and not to harm you, plans to give you hope and a future'" (NIV).

> "I trust in God's Word. He has a plan for me. I may not know what it is, but I know it is the best plan."
> —JAKE

"I trust in God's Word. He has a plan for me. I may not know what it is, but I know it is the best plan. I can live my life knowing I am in God's hand, and he is taking care of me."

3. Listen to the power of your own voice.

A well-intentioned third-grade teacher was trying to teach her class about self-esteem. After she finished her explanation, she wanted to reinforce her lesson and asked anyone in the class to stand who thought they were dumb. At first no one stood. Then a boy in the back stood up. She thought, *Oh no, what do I do now?* So she said, "Johnny, certainly you don't think you are dumb." Johnny said, "No, I'm not dumb. I just didn't want you standing there all by yourself!"

The teacher's inclinations were right to begin with: we are often our worst critics. I don't know what it's like for you, but when most people wake up in the morning and think about their upcoming day, they often engage in "self-talk"—dialogue inside their heads. This self-talk can be negative or positive. For example, negative self-talk could unfold like this: "Oh, I have to meet with Susan today. Every time I meet with her she makes me feel so stupid." Or, "Today is gym class. I don't look nearly as good in shorts as the others in that class."

Self-talk is the endless stream of thoughts that runs through our heads every day. These automatic thoughts can be positive or critical. Some self-talk is well grounded and logical. Other self-talk, however, is based on misconceptions we create.

Negative self-talk based on misconceptions can keep you from moving forward in your way of thinking. It can keep you from making the leap necessary to change. When I was a young boy, I loved to swim. When my friends and I would arrive at the pool, most of us would throw off our clothes and leap ten feet into the deep end of the pool. One of my friends, however, was always worried about the cold temperature of the water. He would run to the shallow end and spend endless minutes putting his feet in until they acclimatized, then his legs up to his knees, then to his waist. Then the cold really hit! You know how it feels when the cold water hits your stomach? Yikes! All the time he was enduring this agony, we were diving, racing, and enjoying the water.

Negative self-talk is similar. You say to yourself, *The water is too cold to jump in*. It affects the way you go about doing things and the way you live your life. When our self-talk takes the form of being destructive, we are held back in our progress. We are frozen without action, and it's action that can help free us to think in new ways and gain the confidence to abandon past impulses.

Following are some simple examples of how we engage in negative self-talk.

Filtering. When we filter, we magnify the negative aspects of a situation and filter out all of the positive ones. For example, you may have done an excellent job at making a presentation to the homeowners association, but you made one minor oversight and forgot to talk about a less important item. That evening in your self-talk, you scold yourself for forgetting something in your presentation, yet you don't even consider how good it was overall.

Personalizing. When we personalize, we immediately assume that if something goes wrong, it must be our fault. Let's say you get a phone call from a client who says he is no longer going to purchase from you. When you personalize, you assume it's because of you, when in fact it may be for myriad reasons not related to you.

Catastrophizing. This is what happens when we assume the worst is going to happen. You think, *If I go to that party, I'll feel stupid because I don't have anything in common with the people there.* Or you assume that if you try something new, it won't work out, so there's no sense in trying at all.

Polarizing. When we polarize our thinking, we see things as one extreme or the other, as black or white, good or bad, perfect or disastrous. In actuality we may have done well at something, but because we polarize, we can't see the good along with the bad. Polarizing is especially harmful when we try to overcome habits and don't recognize our incremental progress. We realize we won't be perfect, so we don't try at all.

What are the consequences of engaging in misguided negative self-talk? One of the most significant is we lose the ability to do the hard things. Hard things are the things that require stepping out of our comfort zones and into the unknown. Hard things stretch our confidence, require a little risk, and even demand some stick-to-it-ive-ness.

We catastrophize our circumstances or polarize our achievements when we engage in negative self-talk. Both are horribly destructive and cause us to run from the hard things.

> To see your potential as God sees your potential, dwell on the good instead of the bad.

How do you overcome negative self-talk tendencies? Practice, practice, practice. Yes, that's right! You have to practice positive self-talk. It may seem strange at first to interrupt your thinking and replace it with something new, but it's critical to changing. If you will practice, you'll find that what was once practice becomes real self-talk that translates into positive action.

To see your potential as God sees your potential, dwell on the good instead of the bad. Have faith in the small blessings God sends your way. Start today to notice even the smallest positive things. When we humbly acknowledge everything good in ourselves, we become more faithful. When we look to God, we become more grateful. We can then see that while we may not have the gifts others have, we have our own gifts that God can use for good. Then God can do great things in our lives, and we can reach our true potential.

In Summary

- To reach our true potential, we have to grow and develop. To do so, we need to see ourselves in a new way.

- Find a trusted friend and read uplifting words to help you see how you can improve.
- Practice positive self-talk.
- Look to God for the reality of who you really are and what you can become.

LEAD FROM THE HEART

*When you cannot make up your mind which of two evenly
balanced courses of action you should take, choose the bolder.*

—GENERAL W. J. SLIM

n the course of sports history, there are only a few teams literally named for their heart. The Cardiac Pack was the name given to the relatively unknown North Carolina State Wolfpack in March 1983.

The heartbeat of the Cardiac Pack was Coach Jim Valvano, recruited from tiny Iona College in 1980. Valvano, outspoken and energetic, landed awkwardly in the elite conservative Atlantic Coast Conference. In the 1980s, the ACC dominated college basketball behind legendary coaches like Dean Smith of North Carolina and Mike Krzyzewski of Duke University. The players in the ACC ruled the court with soon-to-become NBA royalty like Michael Jordon, James Worthy, Ralph Sampson, and Sam Perkins. The young and flamboyant Valvano was different from any other coach in the ACC. He laughed. He smiled. And he wasn't afraid to show his heart.

When Valvano met his players for the first time, he did something unique: he practiced winning. When a team wins the NCAA championship, each player takes his turn climbing atop a ladder and, with scissors in hand, cuts a single strand of the net from the rim. The coach then cuts the final strand, and the team takes the net home as a symbol of victory.

In their first practice and many times over the next four years, Dereck Whittenburg, Thurl Bailey, and the other players practiced the moment in time when they would reach their goals and win a championship. They practiced cutting down the nets. Valvano made them practice everything: raising their fists in the air, cheering in victory, and walking victoriously off the court. At first it seemed odd to set aside the entire practice to cut down the nets, but it soon became the heartbeat of the underdog Wolfpack.

Valvano knew the value of leading with heart. He knew that belief, determination, and imagination were as important as passing, shooting, and rebounding. Over and over again Valvano told them, "I am going to win an NCAA championship." When they lost a game, Valvano would tell them again, "We're going to win a championship."

At the end of the regular season in 1983, despite a winning record, the Wolfpack had lost ten games. There was no possible way they would be invited into the postseason NCAA tournament with ten losses. The only way they could get to the NCAA tournament was to first win the ACC tournament. The winner of the ACC tournament got an automatic bid to the NCAA tournament.

The underdogs from NC State began what has become the most unbelievable nine-game winning streak in college basketball history. In their first game against Wake Forest, they were behind with one minute left to play. They won. Then, against Michael Jordon and North Carolina, they were behind with one minute left. They won. In the ACC Championship game, they came from behind in the final minute to beat Ralph Sampson and Virginia.

They took their come-from-behind winning streak to the NCAA

tournament. Game after game, they were the underdog and found a way to win. After beating Georgia, they were scheduled to play for the NCAA championship against the Houston Cougars, who had an amazing twenty-six-game winning streak. Houston's nickname was Phi Slama Jama. Why? They played "above the rim." It was not uncommon that one-third of their shots were dunks. Hakeem "The Dream" Olajuwon and Clyde "The Glide" Drexler could dazzle the crowd with incredible dunks and showtime moves on the basketball court.

In the second half of the championship game, the Wolfpack found themselves in a familiar position: behind with no chance to win. Then they started their comeback. One defensive stop after another, shot after shot, the score was tied with twenty-four seconds left to play in the game. They played for the last shot. With five seconds to go, Whittenburg took a long three-point shot. It was short, barely reaching the rim. But from the right side of the floor, NC State's Lorenzo Charles jumped up, grabbed the ball, and slammed it into the basket. The Wolfpack won 54-52.

> Valvano taught his players to dream, to practice their victories, and to never give up.

One of the most famous photos in NCAA basketball history is that of Jim Valvano and his team cutting down the nets. Something they had practiced before.

In a matter of a few years, Valvano died of cancer. Before his death he started the V Foundation for Cancer Research. The motto of the V Foundation? "Don't give up . . . Don't ever give up!" Valvano taught his players to dream, to practice their victories, and to never give up.

Jake Olson was a keynote speaker at the fifth annual Dick Vitale's V Foundation for Cancer Research Event held in Sarasota, Florida. Dick Vitale wrote:

I can talk all day long about "never giving up" and The V Foundation, and for those who know me well, there are days I do. Then comes along a 12-year-old boy who personifies our mission and everything we stand for. Jake has demonstrated unbelievable fight in his life. He continues to strive to reach his potential and I love his spirit for battle. I love the fact he is playing competitive golf in high school and continues to fight and raise money for cancer research and to support other children that help. His contribution to The V Foundation, cancer research and his willingness to help others is inspiring.[1]

Like Jim Valvano, leaders with heart are determined. Throughout Jake's fight with cancer, Brian and Cindy Olson have been determined to find a way to win. They simply didn't give up. They coached Jake from the sidelines and helped him imagine his ultimate victory. When they faced setbacks, they helped him find the small miracles along the way.

INSIGHTS FROM JAKE

Though I have many leaders in my life, I will only mention a few. Two of these are my parents. They have always been there for me, giving me support, strength, and love. Not only have they lifted me up during trying times; they have also been there to make the load lighter with a funny story, a joyful moment, or a smile.

My dad has a great sense of humor and a creative imagination. It's a gift I have made my own. We love to expound on everyday events that happen to us. My dad and I can find humor in most situations. Usually a thing or two happens at the golf course, restaurants are usually eventful, and even just walking down the street can turn into an adventure. Sometimes a funny noise or a comment will trigger an array of funny comments. Perhaps it's a function of my hearing and being able to pick up sounds around me. We live in a funny world. When you really stop to notice the funny comments people make or the sounds in the world, you start to appreciate a whole new level of excitement around you.

Keeping a sense of humor during difficult situations is essential to having a positive outlook. I love the fact that my parents have taught me to make lemonade out of sour lemons. I love the fact that we laugh as a family.

My dad is also my personal coach, helping me develop my golf swing. He is the one who takes me to the course or the range. He has been my right-hand man in everything. He always has an answer or a great idea in any situation. He helps me with my homework and explains how to do it.

I admire my dad for his integrity. He does what is right, even if he doesn't benefit from it. He is a man of his word. You can always trust my dad will do what he says he will. He is honest and expects others to be honest also. He cares about me and prays for me every day. We will often read Scripture together and pray. Knowing I have a father who prays for me fills my heart with strength and comfort. I love my dad very much. He has helped me tremendously.

My mom is always there for me as well. She is my biggest fan. She loves me a lot and was with me during all my treatment and hospitalizations. I call her my hospital buddy. We have traveled to and from the hospital more times than anyone can count, and she has been at my side for every single trip. If it is in the middle of the night or if we are going to have to stay there a couple of nights because of treatment, she is there. She has a loving spirit and has taught me love and to be compassionate toward others. She is always looking out for me and making sure I am not getting into trouble.

> I love the fact that we laugh as a family.

My mom is always making sure I eat the right food and that I take my vitamins. She makes sure I am in shape and that nothing is wrong with me physically. Since she is a doctor, I can go to her with any concern about my health. She also cares about my character. She has taught me always to be grateful and to look for the blessings in every situation. Both my parents are amazing people whom I love, trust, and rely on. I thank God for my mom and dad every night.

INSIGHTS FROM BRIAN

Three weeks after losing his sight, Jake was back on the golf course. He struggled with one particular shot more than any other—the chip shot within thirty or forty yards of the green. These were shots that didn't require a full swing, perhaps a soft three-quarter swing or delicate half swing. For these, Jake had a tough time locating the ball. He actually missed it more than he struck it. It wasn't an easy thing to watch. I would be lying if I didn't admit that it brought doubt into my already half-broken heart. It was a harsh reminder that Jake could no longer see. To be honest, golf was not at the top of my list in terms of Jake's future. But it was for Jake. He needed to prove he could do it. I was determined to support him any way I could.

Mike Miles is an accomplished PGA professional and golf teacher out of Virginia Country Club in Southern California. Jake had the opportunity to play with Mike just prior to losing his sight, and Jake told Mike that with or without sight he was not giving up the game. I believe Mike had already suspected this. Without even a blink, Mike offered to help Jake in any way he could and strongly encouraged Jake to come see him at the club whenever he was ready to take his game to the next level. Mike teaches many young golfers and has a genuine heart for the game and for his students.

Jake was excited about his first golf lesson with Mike. Obviously things were different for Jake. Mike worked hard to get him set up over the ball and directionally positioned. Once there, Jake's swing is simply outstanding. Nonetheless, this was a whole new level of challenge. Golf is not an easy game, and playing it without sight is nearly incomprehensible to many. To this day, people ask me, "How does he even do it?" Jake knew he had to learn new skills, new methods, and new ways of playing. Mike knew this too. From the very beginning, he had an inner conviction that Jake could play and play well.

When we arrived for Jake's first lesson, Mike had already determined he was going to start with Jake's pitch shot. So Mike grabbed Jake and led him immediately to the practice chip area and worked on the simple mechanics of hitting a solid pitch. Within minutes, Jake was hitting fairly consistent shots and making some form of contact on nearly every shot.

I can remember on the fourth or fifth shot when Jake hit it as crisp as one can hit it, the sound was as beautiful as any sound I can remember. It just had that clean echo to it as it came off the exact sweet spot on the club. My eyes welled up with tears. I was not really sure why I had an emotional reaction at that moment but have since figured out that it represented a defining moment for Jake; even without sight, he could chip like any golfer. I realized that Mike, in his own mind, had already seen Jake make that swing. Mike already had a vision for Jake making that pitch shot. He had a vision for Jake's potential. In a way, Mike knew a blind person could make that shot. He believed in Jake, and Jake could sense it.

"Mr. Miles has a way of teaching me that works," Jake says. "He teaches from the heart and has a knack for bringing out the best in my swing. I don't always like it and sometimes a small correction doesn't even feel right, but I trust his coaching. He has a belief in me and sees my potential. His sense of the possibilities for me and my game has provided me hope. But most important, he treats me as I imagine he treats any golf student: as a golfer he strives to make better."

Like Coach Miles, leaders with heart are proficient in putting people in the right places and positions to win. They are focused less on what is and more on what could be. They don't wait for the big victory; they're always building on small wins. They affirm and validate. They magnify the truth, beauty, and goodness in others. Their coaching is born from the genuine love they have for their team. That's why God makes such a great coach!

Great coaching, however, is only half of the winning formula. Even with the best coaches, some teams and some players don't win. Why? Winning players also need heart. They need the personal humility necessary to stay coachable and the personal will to stay committed.

The Four Heavies in Leadership

To lead in making a real change, we must lead from the heart. When we lead from the heart, we let who we are, deep down, direct our actions. We aren't easily swayed from our objectives. We aren't governed by our moods. We stop using the leadership behaviors that don't last. We value real change. We are mission oriented.

But as a leader, you not only lead others; you also lead yourself. Perhaps it's time to stop letting life's circumstances lead you and begin leading them. Many of the principles related to leading others apply to leading your own life—principles like decisiveness, professional will, personal humility, maturity, perspective, initiative, and trust. Regardless of whom you're leading, when you lead from the heart, it makes all the difference.

Furthermore, leading has as much to do with what we stop doing as it has to do with what we start doing. It isn't easy. It takes time, investment, and courage. It means you might have to step out of your comfort zone. It requires persistence and patience. Because leading is demanding and time-consuming, when we lead we naturally migrate to what's quick, efficient in the short term, and crisis-ready. We often turn to the four heavies: *manipulation, intimidation, coercion,* and *deceit.*

When We Use Manipulation

We use manipulation to get what we want when other people aren't willing to give it to us. We play on their emotions, work the system, seek to gain an advantage, or use deceptive means to get people to do what they might not have chosen on their own. We present reality the way we want others to see it rather than the way it really is, or try to maintain control and power over others without full disclosure. We rewrite history according to our view and misrepresent things as they really happened.

Rather than lay out the facts plainly and honestly, some leaders use manipulation to hide facts or play on emotion to gain their way. Parents use manipulation when they withhold praise or compliments except when they need something from a child. Then the parent uses praise to generate the desired response from those he is praising. Under this culture, nothing is free; everything is conditional. Withholding praise is one of the most common yet harmful methods of manipulation.

> **If there were only one habit we could teach our children, above all else it would be to give others positive affirmation without the prospect of receiving anything in return.**

As human beings, we are modifiable. Our brains, and the whole human system, are designed to learn and evolve from interacting. Young children and adults will respond to what makes them feel good about themselves. Honest and uplifting feedback given freely without any strings attached creates within us a true sense of self-worth. Compliments given conditionally create falsehood, mistrust, and the sense that "you are only saying that to get me to do what you want."

God asks us to be a light to others. That means we highlight the good in others without the expectation of reciprocity or favor. If there were only one habit we could teach our children, above all else it would be to give others positive affirmation without the prospect of receiving anything in return.

When we lead by regularly shedding light on the strengths and good in others, we gain trust. When we create an atmosphere of trust, we can influence. The result is powerful. Creativity, ideas, teamwork and self-generated hard work are just a few of the outcomes when we lead without manipulation and without withholding our kindness and positive words.

Here's a simple example from a recent column about families:

> David writes a Post-it note to his daughter every night before he goes to bed. He puts it in a place where she will be sure to find it in the morning—on her mirror, in her lunch box, on her bedroom door, or in some other conspicuous place. On each note he writes something he appreciates about her. "I appreciated your help with the dishes tonight" or "I was really inspired by how hard you worked on your math and got an A on your final." One day he went into her room looking for a lost hammer. On his way out he saw 250 Post-it notes stuck on the back of her bedroom door. His daughter had kept every one of his notes. So now, every time she leaves her bedroom she sees 250 notes of appreciation that remind her that somebody loves her. What a powerful message. What wonderful therapy. All from a simple Post-it note.[2]

Intimidation and coercion don't work.

We practice intimidation when we threaten or use our power or position to get others to do what we want them to do. Most common is the use of physical size, stature, or position, but leaders who use intimidation keep others loyal to them by threats of pulling back their support, love, interest, or approval, or by convincing others that they are the only ones with enough experience to give direction.

Intimidation is probably the most frequently used of the four heavies. A department manager uses the threat of dismissal to get what he wants. A parent of young children uses yelling or anger to intimidate. A parent of older children threatens to "make life difficult" to get what she wants. The long-term effect is emotional separation and lack of investment in the relationship. Intimidation works for the moment but only lasts so long.

> The opposite of intimidation is patience, persuasion, and encouragement.

Have you ever been on the receiving end of intimidation? If so, you likely did one thing: withdrew from the relationship. If you didn't get up and leave, you at least mentally and emotionally withdrew. You thought to yourself, *I'll do what he's asking right now, but if there's anything he needs from me in the future, he can forget it!* When we use intimidation or coercion, we lose respect, influence, and willingness. No matter what the relationship, if a leader uses intimidation, the underlying message is always "I am better than you" or "I don't care about you or value your input."

The opposite of intimidation is patience, persuasion, and encouragement. These skills pay big dividends, especially in times of stress and crisis. If you consistently use persuasion and encouragement, in times of crisis you'll have the creativity, teamwork, and loyalty of those with whom you've developed trust. Otherwise you are on your own in times of crisis. They'll do what you say, but that will be the extent others will help you if you haven't laid the foundation of a healthy relationship.

Dump the deceit.

Deceit, in any form, hinders our influence and effectiveness as leaders and parents. I once heard a definition of *dishonesty* that I have always remembered: "Dishonesty is *any* communication with the intent to deceive." We deceive when we leave out important facts, twist words to fit our way, arrange circumstances to favor our version of the truth.

We deceive when we give a false impression, pursue a course contrary to our values or promises we've made, or fail to do what we say we will do. We deceive when we obscure the truth or purposefully leave out known data in order to escape blame or gain a particular end. Leaders, even those with the best intentions, can often find themselves using deception of varying degrees. But when we lead with persuasion and authenticity, we gain freedom and the trust of those we lead.

According to author Robin Lloyd, one of the biggest reasons we deceive is to look good to others and ourselves. In one experiment, psychologist Robert Feldman videotaped two strangers placed in a room as they engaged in a conversation. Following the conversation, each was asked to watch the video and identify anything they said that was "not entirely accurate."

The study, published in the *Journal of Basic and Applied Social Psychology*, showed that 60 percent of participants lied during the conversation with the stranger. On average, they said 2.92 inaccurate things to make themselves look better. Feldman says we deceive because "we want to be agreeable, to make the social situation smoother or easier, and to avoid insulting others through disagreement or discord."[3] Feldman found similar results when testing people in a job-interview situation.

When we are caught being honest, even when it's difficult, we not only gain the trust of those around us, but we increase faith in ourselves. There's something incredibly empowering about being honest no matter what. When we speak the truth and stay true to ourselves by doing what we say we will do, we gain greater peace. As Socrates said, "The greatest way to live with honor in this world is to be what we pretend to be."

When children or spouses feel lied to or manipulated, they assume love, affirmation, and authentic concern are conditional. In this environment, all things seem temporary and insecure. As a result, the manipulated look elsewhere for feelings of importance and genuine love.

Believe it or not, we use these four heavy propositions when leading our own lives as well. We tell ourselves that we're just not as good as another person so we shouldn't even try. That's an untruth. That's pure deceit. We manipulate our lives by engaging in rationalization, making things that aren't true seem like truth to give ourselves a temporary respite from difficulties.

> "The greatest way to live with honor in this world is to be what we pretend to be."
>
> —SOCRATES

As leaders or parents, we turn to the four heavies when things are stressful or in times of crisis. The problem is that with many organizations and families in continual crisis, these four heavy propositions are used over and over again. After continual use, they become less and less effective. For the leaders who use them repeatedly, they become habit. And, with continual use, they soon become the only behavior that some leaders possess.

Using these heavy propositions, in any degree, erodes the trust necessary for constructive personal and organizational change. The usual reaction by people who are on the receiving end of one of the four heavies is to engage in survival strategies, defensiveness, alienation, entrenchment, positioning, fear, and learned helplessness. That's why organizations in continual crisis lose many of their best employees. They're too tired of the heavies.

For example, when people experience coercion in an organization or from their boss, their internal response might be, "I'm just going to keep a low profile until my boss's mood changes or I can transfer to another department." As a result, open feedback comes to a halt, creativity goes by the wayside, and no one dares offer an opinion as to how to improve. In response to intimidation, defensiveness and alienation emerge in the organization. Employees shift from long-term thinking to short-term survival. Side conversations start up and gossip prevails. The side conversations construct organization culture and erode the leader's reputation. Trust departs and apathy takes over.

Out with the Old and in with the New

On one of the more famous episodes of *Seinfeld*, George Costanza is convinced his judgment is permanently flawed. He believes his instincts are always wrong. One day, he says to Jerry, "It became very clear to me sitting out there today that every decision I've made in my entire life has been wrong. My life is the complete opposite of everything I want it to be. Every instinct I have, in every aspect of life, be it something to wear, something to eat—it's all been wrong."[4] So George decides to do the opposite of whatever he would naturally do.

He goes into the diner and, instead of ordering his usual item off the menu, he pauses, thinks, and orders the exact opposite. When his food is delivered, he notices a beautiful woman looking his way. His normal reaction would be not to talk to her because he was afraid. But instead, he does the opposite: he talks to her. She had noticed him because his out-of-the-ordinary lunch order was the same as hers. He asks her out and she agrees. That begins a spree of fortuitous events each time he chooses the opposite of what his instincts tell him to do.

Sometimes, when your leadership isn't going like you want, follow George's example and choose the opposite. If you've been leading with manipulation or any of the four heavies, choose the opposite. If you've been lecturing too much, choose the opposite. The opposite of manipulation is empowerment. Engage in dialogue, and let others arrive at their own conclusions.

Think Dialogue, Not Discourse

Leading with dialogue is not easy or quick. With dialogue you believe the solutions exist and that someone on your team has the solution. Your job is to help them find it. So you engage in dialogue to help them discover the right way. You don't set yourself up as the expert. You become more of a facilitator.

James Belasco and Ralph Stayer wrote a national best seller entitled *Flight of the Buffalo* in which they contrast a herd of buffalo with a flock of geese. Buffalo follow a single leader. When the lead buffalo moves, they move in a single file. As a result, they're constantly watching the leader to determine their next move, and he is constantly under duress to look out for danger. In contrast, geese fly in a V shape and they take turns flying in the lead position. They all participate in determining the right direction to travel. When you lead from the heart, everyone gets a chance to lead.

> When you lead from the heart, everyone gets a chance to lead.

Leading by dialogue is a lot like flying in a "V" formation. Leaders don't have to be in the lead position all the time. Through positive and affirmative questions, they allow others to reach their own conclusions. They create leaders and develop the potential in others.

In the family setting, the easiest thing is for a parent to give direction, to lecture from his or her position of authority. However, dialogue requires that a parent ask questions, listen to the answers, and have a great sense of timing. Dialogue takes time but ultimately saves time because it develops skills in other people.

In a dialogue you:

- ask questions and resist the temptation to lecture
- are sensitive to others' feelings, hopes, and ideas
- listen to others to understand and build alignment
- search for the best idea, not just your idea
- see all sides of an issue
- invite continuous feedback

When you lead with dialogue, others are less likely to feel alienated, fearful, entrenched, or defensive. They have no need to actively protect their positions and engage in gamesmanship and are able to act more freely and openly. They make their own choices as they themselves develop. And you learn and grow as the leader because you're open to new ideas and feedback. Trust increases between children and parents because children feel respect.

I've learned the best time to teach as a parent is when it's *not* teaching time. And the worst time to teach is when it *is* teaching time. Let me explain. Let's say your teenage son comes home after the agreed-upon time one night. You've been waiting up and you're tired. He knows you're going to be waiting up for him and you're going to be upset. You're thinking, *It's time to teach him a lesson*. But it's the wrong time.

Don't get me wrong. There should be consequences. He may lose use of the cell phone or not be able to drive the car for a few days, but it's not time to teach. He won't really learn from your teaching when you're handing out consequences at 1:00 a.m. Wait a few days. When you're driving down the road together on your way to the golf course, tell him what you've learned in life. Tell him how important morality and obedience are to you. Tell him why you feel that way. Let him hear from you the good things that come in life from making good choices. Talk about how proud you are that he often makes the right choices.

Tell him a story from your youth. Remember, this is a dialogue, not a lecture. It starts with a question or two, and then you get an opportunity to share what you've learned.

Another perfect time to teach is when your children come home on time. We, as parents, often notice when our children come home late, but do we ever thank them when they come home on time? I've learned some of the best discussions in life with teenagers happen at midnight. If parents are relaxed and willing to talk, a teenager will go on and on talking for hours. You'll lose sleep but you'll gain a friend. Think about it. If your teenager has a really great talk with you when he comes home on time, will he come home on time more often? You bet. I know a mother who bakes hot chocolate chip cookies and has them out of the oven at midnight when her son is supposed to be home. He walks in the door, gets a cookie, and she calmly asks how he's doing. Then she sits back and lets him talk. Leading with dialogue—or even cookies—works!

It's no different at work. I've learned the best time to teach is not in a crisis. The best time to teach is when you can affirm, not correct. Each month I ask department heads to bring their teams and sit down for a scorecard meeting. We call them scorecard meetings, but to myself, I call them affirmation meetings. I do that to remind myself that my job is to affirm, not to lead. In these meetings, they report their progress toward their goals, brag on their accomplishments for the month, and tell me what they're going to do next month to improve and reach their goals.

I've learned that in this session I don't talk very much. My first tendency is to teach and expound using my "vast" knowledge. You may be the same. If so, resist that temptation. Let them talk. Ask affirmative questions, like, "What did you learn when you made those changes?" Tell them what you love about what they did. Use those exact words: "Let me tell you what I love about what you did . . ." In my experience, as you talk about what went wrong and what went right, nine times out of ten, they will reach the same conclusion you would reach, and they did it on their own.

If these scorecard meetings have an affirmative tone and are done in a dialogue format, your people will learn to lead. They'll engage in a process of continuous improvement. Your teaching in this format is exponentially more effective.

Potentiating Leadership

Our leadership style changes when we care more about the person than the immediate outcome. And I've learned that when we do, we eventually get a better outcome. How? We create ownership, capability, and trust.

Most people will look to someone else for direction. Why? It's easier. We've been trained to think that way. We look to the government to solve our economic crisis, we look to our spouses to bring more love into our relationship, or we look to our boss to have the answers. The truth is, we're very good at avoiding leadership.

When it comes to leading, we've become rescuers rather than enablers. If something goes wrong at work, we step in to solve the problem. If something goes wrong with one of the kids, we jump in with all the solutions. When we do, we're not creating capability in others.

Brian Tracy tells the story of the construction worker who "opens up his lunch box at the noon break and unwraps his sandwich to find that it contains sardines. He gets really upset and complains loudly to everyone around him about how much he hates sardines. The next day, the same thing happens: a sardine sandwich. Again, the construction worker shouts and complains about how much he hates sardines for lunch. The third day it happens again. By this time, his fellow workers are getting fed up with his loud complaining. One of them leans over and says to him, 'If you hate sardines so much, why don't you tell your wife to make you some other kind of sandwich?' The construction worker turns to the fellow and says, 'Oh, I'm not married. I make my own lunches!'" As leaders, our job is to help others take responsibility.

I refer to leaders who focus on people first. People are our most valuable asset. Our job as leaders is to increase the value of that asset and help them improve. The first lesson a potentiating leader learns is the person doing the work must take the responsibility. If you have an employee who doesn't want or isn't able to take full responsibility, help him. Coach him. If he still won't take responsibility, coach him again. But if after repeated coaching, nothing changes, get a new employee. You can't continually fix him. Nothing is more energy draining. Get the right people and get the right focus.

How do you get employees to take responsibility? Set clear and realistic expectations. Write them down. Then set up time for regular accountability. Remember your focus as a leader is to help them develop. Resist the urge to rescue. Resist the temptation to do it yourself.

In today's society one of the most difficult transitions for a family is when children go from high school to college. They go from living at home to living on their own. They have to learn how to take 100 percent responsibility for their lives. It's a big adjustment. For whatever reason, our kids today seem to have a mistaken sense of entitlement. They think they are entitled to a cell phone. They believe they're entitled to a gym membership, and they shouldn't have to work to pay for it. They shouldn't have to work to have nice things in life.

If you're like me, I reflect back on my college days and think, *My parents didn't give me those things. I had to work. I had a job when I was going to school.* Why do our kids believe they shouldn't have to? Because we've allowed them to continue to think that way! If we were focused on their potential, then we'd let them learn the hard way more often, and we wouldn't step in to rescue them every time they hurt or are hungry.

When our children started going to college, my wife and I decided they were going to be responsible for paying for housing, gas, and living expenses. They would have to work part-time while going to school, or work during the summer months to be able to pay for living expenses during the year.

During his first semester, my son decided not to work while he was going to school. He was in a baseball league that practiced every afternoon. He didn't have time to play baseball, work, and study for his classes. So he quit his afternoon job to make room for baseball. He had a little money saved up, but not enough to last the entire semester. Sure enough, with six weeks left in the semester, he ran out of money. He had no food. What was the first thing he did? He called home. He explained how hungry he was and how he had no money for gas in the car. We listened, but we didn't rescue him. When he finally realized we weren't sending any money, he did what any person would do: he cried. We listened some more, but we didn't rescue him. Soon enough, he had a job again.

Potentiating leaders are naturally forward looking. This requires a good sense of intuition. Potentiating leaders work with a sense of purpose but are not overly urgent in their approach with people. They match their pace to the development capabilities of others. This patience is rooted in an understanding that failure is a powerful teacher and sometimes we need time to fail forward.

Potentiating leaders are always working on vision. They're gifted noticers and are always pointing out the potential. They inspire. As Stephen Covey said, "Leadership is communicating to people their worth and potential so clearly that they come to see it in themselves."[5]

That doesn't mean we're overly patient. Good leaders don't nudge things along; they move things along. At the same time, potentiating leaders are empathetic because they are imperfect learners themselves. They don't yield to destructive impulses like blaming, avoiding, complaining, or labeling. They see with inner conviction what other people can actually become. When others feel that we believe in them, our dialogue takes on a different character. It's more alive and authenticity prevails.

INSIGHTS FROM JAKE

When I think of someone who is a true potentiating leader, I immediately think of Coach Carroll. I admire Coach Carroll on so many levels. He is not just a great coach; he's also a great human being. He is real with his players, real with the fans, true to the game, and true to himself. Coach is not shy about driving his players hard and is unwilling to stop short of bringing out the very best in each of them. He coaches them from a place of wanting the best for them. Yes, Coach Carroll wants to win, but the philosophy he brings to the locker room is about getting his players to be true to themselves in practicing, competing, and living. If they win, that's great, but that's not what his philosophy is about.

In his recent book *Win Forever,* Coach Carroll reveals his philosophy on reaching your potential: "If you want to win forever, always compete."[6] Coach Carroll believes that you are either competing or you're not, and that anyone can choose to be a great competitor at whatever they are doing in life.

Coach's *Win Forever* philosophy includes points such as no complaining, respect everyone, everything counts, practice hard, and expect to win. It is a philosophy that has brought him tremendous success. But I would respectfully add that *Win Forever* doesn't directly address Coach Carroll's most powerful coaching principle, the glue that holds his philosophy together: his genuine love for the game, the team, and the players individually. Within the book, Coach Carroll humbly dances around it by identifying principles such as taking care of the team first, coaching as a teacher, and having fun. But he loves the game and he loves people.

Coach Carroll's passion is contagiously powerful. It's what makes players want to play hard, compete, and perform. Each knows that Coach Carroll cares for him as a person, not just as a player. I experienced this care firsthand. The care he showed for me is something that will remain with me forever. It was authentic and genuine. It was inspiring! He leads from the heart, and trusts his own instincts in carrying out his coaching duties.

Coach Carroll's winning attitude is amazing. He expects to win. It's not arrogance; it's simply a mind-set that says when he takes the football field or the field of life, he expects to be a winner. Coach instills this winning attitude in his players and his coaching staff. Circumstances and challenges may arise, and one may not always win, but the game of football and the game of life cannot be truly played without a heart of a champion. Coach Carroll is a master at nourishing the mind-set of a champion.

Lead with Courage

Laid to rest in the Pine Grove Cemetery in Brunswick, Maine, is a former governor of Maine who, when he was elected in 1866, received the highest percentage of votes ever received by a governor before or since in the state of Maine. Governor Joshua Chamberlain was not only popular but also respected by those he served.

Born in Brewer, Maine, Chamberlain was the oldest of five children. He graduated from Brunswick College in 1852, married Fanny Adams in 1855, and began his career as a professor of modern languages. With the outbreak of the Civil War, Chamberlain volunteered for service. He rejected appointment as a colonel, preferring to start at a lower rank and "learn the business." At the battles of Fredericksburg and Chancellorsville, Chamberlain properly earned the rank of colonel.

Chamberlain was made famous by his leadership at the battle of Gettysburg. On the second day of the battle, Confederate forces assembled into positions below a line of hills south of the town. They began to attack the Union's left flank, which was atop a small slope called Little Round Top. Chamberlain found himself and the Twentieth Maine, which he commanded, at the far left end of the entire Union line, directly in harm's way.

Given his battle experience, Chamberlain understood the need to hold the left flank at all costs. The men from Maine waited. The Alabama Fifteenth attacked the left flank relentlessly. Time and time again the Confederates struck, until the Twentieth Maine had incurred high casualties and exhausted their supply of ammunition. Colonel Chamberlain recognized the dire circumstances. Without ammunition they could not withstand another charge. He ordered his boys on the left wing to fix bayonets and prepare for a charge. This was an unexpected move.

Upon his command, the Twentieth Maine charged down the hill, with the left wing swinging inward like a hinge. The Confederate army was caught off guard by the unexpected move; many soldiers surrendered. The courageous maneuver served as a catalyst to turn the tide of the battle.

> Courage inspires. Courage lifts. Courage engages our sense of duty, leading us to do what we might not otherwise do on our own.

When we lead with faith, we play offense instead of defense. Chamberlain acted with faith, not fear. If we think about leading from the heart, there are times when we, too, need to "fix bayonets." Leading with courage brings feelings of initiative, hope, and energy.

Courage inspires. Courage lifts. Courage engages our sense of duty, leading us to do what we might not otherwise do on our own. We often forget the impact our own example has on those we lead, but we lead by example whether we intend to or not. When we exercise courage in our own lives, even in small ways, we inspire others to do the same.

INSIGHTS FROM JAKE

When my parents first learned I had cancer, we prayed for God to remove it. What God did was send us one miracle after another. When we went to the hospital, we met a woman named Nancy Mansfield. She became my advocate and friend as I went through all the treatment and surgeries over the next twelve years. Nancy truly loved me. She would fight for my rights at the hospital and ensure that I was getting the best treatment and best doctors. She would sing to me while I waited for my surgeries; she would play with me during the long hours waiting for tests. When I had to go to New York for an experimental treatment, she called me several times a day to make sure things were going all right. When I had to be rushed to the hospital with a high fever at midnight, she met us there. She not only cared about me but about my entire family. Nancy made sure Emma was being taken care of during this time. The day I had my last eye removed, Nancy made sure I had my favorite anesthesiologist, my favorite nurse, paved the way for Kris O'Dowd to be there, and, of course, for Dr. Murphree to do the surgery.

Before the surgery, we all gathered around and prayed. It was very comforting. Nancy told us we were going to be okay. She was right. After I became blind, Nancy bought me a guitar for Christmas. She intuitively knew I would be good at it and that it would be healing for me. She helped connect me to other people who could help me with my blindness. She was always thinking of ways to improve our lives and the lives of the other children she helped. I called her my guardian angel here on earth.

Nancy unexpectedly passed away in November 2010. At the memorial, I eulogized Nancy's contribution to our family:

Our family has reserved a special place in our hearts for Nancy. Yes, Nancy had a gift for helping families. She stood her ground despite worry, fear, and devastation. It was mainly due to her ability to not just be compassionate, but rather stand right in the middle of the storm, joining forces with the family, letting her heart and spirit be vulnerable and wounded. It was this level of humanity that made Nancy special to the world around her. May God continue to bless her long-lasting impact on the families she touched.

I miss her, and the world will miss her loving contribution.

In Summary

- Leadership makes things happen. We need to lead our lives to make things happen.
- Do you use the four heavies of leadership? The four heavies erode trust and credibility.
- When we engage in dialogue instead of discourse and magnify the potential in others, we cultivate trust and credibility.
- Lead from within. Focus on how to serve first, and all other things will follow.

A HABIT OF HAPPINESS

We are what we repeatedly do. Excellence,
then, is not an act but a habit.

—WILL DURANT

egend has it that the *touchstone* was a small pebble that could turn any common metal into pure gold. A poor man, who discovered the legend of the touchstone from parchment hidden in an ordinary book, learned that the touchstone was lying among thousands of other pebbles on the shores of the Black Sea. So he sold all he had and camped on the seashore to look for the pebble.

The legend said one could tell the difference between the touchstone and the other pebbles because the touchstone, unlike regular pebbles, was warm instead of cold to the touch.

This poor man spent his days picking up pebbles, testing whether they were cold or warm. Feeling them to be cold, he would then toss them into the sea; he didn't want to drop them on the shore and have to sort through them again. Every day for weeks and months, he continued picking up pebbles and tossing them into the surf.

One morning he picked up a pebble and it was warm to his touch, but out of habit and before he could take it back, he tossed it into the sea. The touchstone was never to be found again.

Like this poor man, the same thing happens with habits in our lives. We miss out on great things because we have habits of living certain ways. Our habits keep us from the things that would make us happy. We haven't developed a habit of happiness.

Nothing shapes our personalities more than habit. For example, let's say you're stressed and in a hurry, and because you're always busy, the stress never stops. As a result, you have little time for people. As this pattern persists, you develop the habit of being cold and detached. Soon it's easier for you to avoid others than to make the effort to be friendly. You know you should be friendly, but being cold has become comfortable. It's second nature. It's habit. As a result, your coworkers avoid you whenever possible. You, in return, avoid them. Friendships you have forged over the years begin to fade. What began as stress and a busy schedule has turned into a way of life without the company of people you care about.

How do you reverse the habit? Smile when you see others, use a warm tone of voice when you speak to them, and purposefully slow down. Rearrange your schedule to set aside time so as not to be in a hurry with those you love. Pretty soon, the habit of smiling starts to become part of who you are inside.

Being happy is also a habit. Most people think being happy is something that happens to them rather than something they choose to be. In life, we constantly check to see if we *feel* happy, when in fact, we can choose to *be* happy. People with a happy disposition still face difficulties in life, but they tend to be happier in the process.

The truth is, when we roll out of bed in the morning and face a new day, we have a simple choice: be in a good mood or a bad mood. We get to choose what makes us happy. We can choose how we react to others. We can choose to smile. We can choose how we'll live.

INSIGHTS FROM JAKE

Blindness can definitely generate moments of frustration. One of my bigger frustrations is trying to find things, such as my drinking glass (especially when someone moves it), the TV remote, or my shoes. Just looking for an object can take fifteen or twenty minutes. I have to feel everything and put a lot of time and effort into doing the simplest of tasks. I have learned to be patient and content. It might take me thirty minutes to figure out how to do my homework on my braille notebook or I'll get lost trying to get somewhere and have to start from the beginning again. I know I'll eventually do what I set out to do if I'm patient and persevere. I also have to be careful walking around because people leave things in the middle of the floor or leave cabinet doors open, and then I run into them.

Running into an open cabinet door definitely makes me feel grumpy. I get frustrated in the moment. I also get frustrated when I can't figure out the direction that I need to be heading in, so I have to ask for help. I don't like asking for help because it gives me the feeling of failure. I don't like being dependent on people.

Then I have to realize that this is my life, and complaining about this stuff will not get me anywhere. Instead, I have to face it and find a solution. Complaining is a waste of time and does not solve anything. It keeps you focused on the negative. Facing my problems with a will to find solutions gives me hope and empowerment and lets me take charge of my own life. Then I don't feel so grumpy because I know I can do something about it.

Living with Less Stress

Science is learning more and more every day about the impact of prolonged stress to our thinking and health. When we experience a temporary threat, our body gives us a temporary boost in adrenaline and immediate stress response. This response allows us to focus, creates energy, and elevates our response mechanisms. Sometimes we like stress because it kicks in our ability to focus. Like an addict, however, we soon begin to rely on the feeling of stress to initiate any difficult or slightly difficult daily activity. Out of habit and without thinking, we even manufacture stress before doing a difficult task.

The body doesn't distinguish between physical and psychological threats. It can't tell whether you're stressed over a busy schedule or if someone is holding a gun to your face. Your physical systems react the same way. If you have a lot of worries and your life is constantly in "hurry" mode, then your emergency stress response is activated most of the time. And the more your body's stress system is activated, the harder it is to shut it off. Over the long term, this chronic exposure to stress begins to disrupt many of your important health systems.

But not only are there detrimental health effects, like higher blood pressure, lower immune function, and increased risk of heart disease, the effect on the brain is also substantial. Stress decreases the number of connections made in the brain. Over time, this impacts ongoing brain function. It slows brain connections and our ability to learn new things. When we're constantly stressed, we think more narrowly and lack the ability to think as creatively as we otherwise might.

Breaking free from the tight grip that stress has on our lives isn't easy, but it's essential to a habit of happiness. Like flying an airplane, you have several essential controls that can elevate your ability to deal with stress.

Sense of control

When you feel that you're not in control of your life, your stress levels increase. Conversely, when you have confidence in your ability to direct your life and persevere through difficult things, or when you have help to take on the tough challenges, you have less stress.

How do you gain this sense of control? Exercise faith: faith in yourself, in your support system, and in God. Even if you aren't sure you can prevail, have faith that you will, with help. This assurance gives you the peace you need to act without anxiety or fear.

Support network

Rely on a support network of friends and family. A trusted support network can buffer the daily trials that might otherwise cause undue stress. A support network allows you a place to turn for strength, encouragement, and help.

Most importantly, be a support for others. It's amazing the stress we relieve from our own lives when we are helping others. We gain confidence to face our own trials and better perspective on what's most important. Love pushes the stress out of our lives.

> Love pushes the stress out of our lives.

Sense of humor

Nothing relieves stress like optimism and laughter. A husband and wife were each celebrating their sixtieth birthdays, which happened to be on the same day. A wealthy uncle had sent them an antique lamp from his collection of treasures as a birthday present. Inside the lamp was a genie who suddenly appeared and granted them each one wish.

The wife said, "I love to travel, but my grumpy husband doesn't. We haven't even traveled outside our state! I wish for my husband to travel with me around the world!" Immediately, *poof*, two round-the-world tickets appeared in her hand.

Bothered, the husband wasn't going to be outdone. "Fine," he said. "Then I want to travel with a beautiful woman thirty years younger than me." And *poof*, he was ninety years old.

Make laughter a part of your daily life. Make a few jokes. Share a funny story. Learn to laugh. When we laugh at a situation, we let go of things that might otherwise accumulate in our thinking and get in the way of life.

One day I saw my neighbors walking down the street, hand in hand, laughing as they walked along. A few days later, I ran into them and told them I had seen them and said that they had looked so happy. They told me their only car had broken down that day. The repair bill was more than the car was worth, so they just walked away from it. Worst of all, he had been laid off from his job that morning. Both things happened on the same day! They decided that all they could do was laugh. Both situations were out of their control, and there was nothing to do but smile and move on. They not only walked away from their car; they walked away from their stress as well.

Preparation

If we're prepared, there's no need to stress. When we're prepared, we can work through life's challenges without disruption. To be prepared, have a plan. Know where you're headed. It's just like when you're going on a trip. If you know your end destination, you might get a flat tire, but that flat tire isn't going to keep you from your goal. You'll just fix the tire and keep going. If you don't have a plan, a flat tire might keep you from going any farther.

Anticipate what might happen. It's easier to approach new things in life once you've already considered them in your mind. It's like you've already gone for a test drive. After that, the actual drive is pretty easy. Planning informs your decision making. The more you know about a stressful situation, the easier it is to deal with it. For example, imagine you are going to have surgery. If you're familiar with the procedure and recovery time, you'll be able to anticipate and leave much of the stress of the event behind.

Focus on what matters most

When we are focused on what matters most, we don't dwell on the things that matter least. We're able to let things go. We abandon even good ideas if they aren't as great as the priority we've chosen. There's great peace in life when we let go of distraction and choose to move forward toward our hopes and dreams.

INSIGHTS FROM CINDY

I thought running a business and raising twins was a lot to handle until Jake was diagnosed with cancer. Nothing could prepare me for the long trips to the hospital, the countless hours spent there, and the stress of waiting for the latest news on Jake's cancer.

When Jake was diagnosed at eight months old, I watched helplessly as he was put under anesthesia over and over again so the doctor could perform tests and give him treatments. Each procedure came with the risk that Jake wouldn't survive. I prayed too many times to count. I sat with him for days while an IV pole fed toxic chemo drugs into his frail little body. He lost his hair and was so sick. How could my little boy survive it?

Our first Christmas with our twins was spent in the hospital emergency room and oncology ward because Jake's blood counts plummeted and he got a severe infection. Brian and I sat next to his tent-covered crib and prayed for God to spare his life.

Over the next twelve years, Jake's cancer returned again and again. Every time was a fight. Every treatment was fraught with risk. But the treatments were just part of the battle. In the days during and after treatments, Jake would vomit violently because of the chemo drugs. I gave him daily injections to help his low blood counts recover. He missed so many things because he was sick and unable to get out of bed. He missed parties, events, and playing with his friends. So did we. His cancer robbed our family of the normal things families get to do. The stress of everyday living combined with all that comes with cancer was overwhelming to me.

I quickly learned I couldn't handle the stress on my own. I needed God's help. I prayed, wrote in my journal, read God's Word, and surrounded myself with loving family and friends. I started reciting verses from the Bible that reinforced God's love for me. As I did, I learned to give all my heartache and worry to God. I learned to trust in him. Matthew 6:25–34 tells us that God says not to worry. His promises are sure. He will give us his strength to handle the trials in our lives.

To better handle stress, I learned my body needed exercise. Exercise releases brain chemicals that help us feel happier. And having a support team is essential. Our family, friends, and church helped with meals, rides, and encouragement. As Jake grew older, he would ask to stop by our church and pray with our pastor when we received news about his cancer. Jake got great comfort from praying with the pastor and staff. He knew God was present and on his side.

Happiness Is Contagious

Can we catch happiness like we catch a cold? Studies show that happiness and unhappiness rub off on others. In one study, students randomly assigned to a mildly depressed roommate became increasingly depressed over a three-month period. James Fowler and Nicholas Christakis studied the effect our happiness has on others. Their research shows that emotional states can be "transferred directly from one individual to another by mimicry and emotional contagion."[1] We copy the emotional state and facial expressions we see in others.

Studies show that happiness and unhappiness rub off on others.

Fowler and Christakis proved happiness spreads not only directly, but even indirectly—through friends of friends. Using happiness and depression measurements, and sophisticated network analysis, they demonstrated that happy people created clusters of happy people around them. They used network analysis and mapping to show that when happy people move into a neighborhood, over time those around them become happier as well.

Each person has a natural disposition, which dictates a particular level of optimism, cheerfulness, and inclination to be happy. Certainly the influence of others makes a big difference in the choice to be happy. Our children take their cues from us. If we complain, they complain. If we're happy, they're happy. One thing is certain: the happier we are, the happier the people in our lives become.

If *others* can influence your happiness, *you* can also influence your happiness. You have a choice. You can choose a happier habit, and that habit can carve deep trenches in your way of thinking and behaving.

Recently, I heard the story of a farmer who raised pigeons as a hobby. He loved his birds and would go to great lengths naming each one after a characteristic that he noticed in its personality. One pigeon in particular caught his eye. The bird rarely kept up with the others when in flight. He named the bird Too Slow.

One day after releasing the birds, the farmer watched in dismay as a hawk swept down on the pigeons and found Too Slow flying behind the others. The hawk attacked in midair, and the hawk and pigeon tumbled to the earth as feathers floated to the ground. The farmer ran to the spot where he saw them fall, but neither the hawk nor Too Slow could be found.

Presuming that Too Slow was dead, the farmer returned home. A few days later, Too Slow returned, a few feathers missing but still alive. The farmer nursed him back to health, and a few weeks later Too Slow rejoined the other pigeons in their flight together. This time Too Slow wasn't too slow. He stayed squarely in the middle of the group. He wasn't in front or in back. Too Slow had learned his lesson.

We can learn the same way. If we keep doing what we've been doing, then we'll keep getting what we've been getting. But if we haven't been happy, then we can change what we've been doing. Our habits can change. We can choose to be happy.

INSIGHTS FROM JAKE

Sometimes we're afraid of letting things go in life. We're afraid of change. I sometimes have to laugh when I think about the times when I heard my parents or friends complain about spraining their thumb or finger and losing the use of it for a while. I have heard them say, "Wow, I didn't realize how much I used this finger until I lost the use of it." Try losing your sight! You just don't realize how much you use it until you lose it.

The transition to blindness has been difficult to say the least. But like everything else, transitioning and learning new skills takes practice and time. When I first became blind I had no clue how to get around, how to read Braille, or even how to know when my glass was full of water when I was filling it up. At first, everything was a challenge. The simplest of things (finding my toothbrush, knowing where the furniture was located, determining which clothes I was grabbing) became very difficult. There were a couple of days early on that I went to school wearing one black sock and one white sock, or I wore my shirt inside out the whole day. Actually, I am not even sure that has anything to do with blindness, as I probably did that before losing my sight as well. But finding a car door handle, plugging a plug into an outlet, knowing where the food is on my plate, and playing the guitar have all been learning experiences. It has required effort and patience, but at the end of the day it all works.

It seems that when I lost my sight, all my other senses kicked into high gear. I can hear, smell, touch, and sense better than other people. I can hear where other people are in the house. I can sense when I am approaching someone on the sidewalk. I can hear conversations and quickly identify a familiar voice. My sense of smell has improved. I can feel when my water glass is full or if I have food on my fork. Additionally, I have gained an appreciation for talk radio, and I love to listen to sporting events. I have made a habit of listening to the Bible through my CD player.

None of this has taken away from the joy of actually being at events. I still love going to football games and being in the crowd, or going to church and being in the main auditorium, or going to professional golf events. I went to the U.S. Open at Pebble Beach and was at the course every day taking it all in. I could sense the action, feel the tension, and hear the roars of the crowds. It was awesome.

I also enjoy meeting new people. I can generally tell a lot about a person by his handshake, the sound of his voice, and the projection of his speech. I know how tall he is, his age, and his general demeanor. It is amazing how much our other senses can tell us.

I am still able to write the words you're reading now. I don't use a pen and paper or a computer, like most writers, I use a device called a BrailleNote that allows me to type in Braille. The device reads back what I wrote, and at the same time I can feel the words I wrote in Braille. It is extremely efficient, and I have mastered it. The BrailleNote also helps me in school with taking notes, studying, and doing my homework.

I have learned new ways to do math, algebra, and calculus through specialized devices and methods. I have done so well in algebra that I received one of the highest entrance grades in math for my high school placement test, completed honors algebra, and am currently taking honors calculus.

Of course, there are bigger things to worry about, such as knowing where the stairs start and stop, crossing a street, or running into things that are just waiting for me! It took a little while to find different tricks to help me avoid the bumps and bruises.

I've become proficient with my cane and learned echo location, which enables me to use a clicking sound to identify objects (similar to what dolphins use in the ocean). I've improvised in other areas as well. I play soccer with a plastic bag over the ball so I can hear where the ball is traveling. I put pieces of tape on the back of my guitar that align with the third, fifth, seventh, ninth, and twelfth frets so I can move my hand to them quicker. I can throw a football to someone as long as he claps his hands.

I normally play center and long snapper for my football team, which has required me to listen keenly for where the defensive players line up and move to. My touchdown pass was a onetime event, one pass and one touchdown, so I have a better pass rating than most pro quarterbacks: a 100 percent completion rating with one touchdown and no interceptions!

It's funny that when you lose things in your life, you find other things that make your life more rich and rewarding.

The Set of the Soul

Ella Wheeler Wilcox said it best:

> One ship drives east and another drives west,
> With the self-same winds that blow,
> 'Tis the set of the sails
> And not the gales
> That tells us the way to go.
> Like the winds of the sea are the ways of fate,
> As we voyage along through life,
> 'Tis the set of a soul
> That decides its goal
> And not the calm, or the strife.[2]

It's the set of our soul that decides the calm or the strife. When we set our courses to be better, even in little ways, we set our dispositions to be more positive. It's almost impossible to be working toward a worthy goal and still holding on to past mistakes or thinking of why we are unhappy. When we are working toward our goals, we find new pathways we may never have traveled in life.

In 2007, a smart, beautiful young lady named Rachel Smith from

Clarksville, Tennessee, won the Miss USA pageant. She had graduated magna cum laude from Belmont University in Nashville. She
worked for years to earn her title as Miss Tennessee and then Miss
USA. That May, she would compete in the Miss Universe pageant in
Mexico.

Rachel arrived in Mexico City on May 1, 2007, with the other
seventy-seven delegates from countries around the world. After competing in the preliminary competition, Smith made the semifinal
round along with fourteen other women. In the semifinals, the top
fifteen women competed in three events. Rachel did well in the first
two events. Then came the evening gown competition. She and the
other contestants prepared every detail. She had practiced her walk
hundreds of times. As she started her walk onto the stage, the worst
possible thing happened: she slipped, her legs flew out from under her,
and she fell flat on her backside before quickly jumping up and resum-
ing her walk, trying her best to remain as composed as she possibly
could. This was a disaster. Everything she had worked for was gone in
a single second.

Despite her fall, she made it into the top five finalists. During the
final question-and-answer competition, with the local crowd booing
and millions of people watching, she was asked a question randomly
selected by the judges. The question was this: "If you could go back
and relive one moment of your life, what moment would you pick and
why?"

Well, of course, she would have liked a do-over in the evening gown
competition, right? But that wasn't her answer. Without hesitation,
Rachel said if she could relive any moment of her life again, she would
relive her trip to South Africa, where she volunteered and worked with
young girls.

Rather than choose a point in her past when she was disappointed,
Rachel chose a time when she was happiest. She chose to dwell on a
moment of joy rather than disappointment.

When you're in pursuit of something worthwhile, you don't drag along the "should haves" in your life. You give yourself permission to let go without guilt or anxiety. You don't worry about what you've lost, only about what you're gaining.

Jake had to let go of some pretty important things in his life. I've noticed he doesn't spend much time looking back on when he lost his sight, or even asking why. He turns and faces the future with courage and enthusiasm.

Being happy is a matter of choice and habit. You can be happy despite circumstances. You can simplify your life, lose the gloom, change your outlook, and live closer to God. By doing so, you'll find the habit of happiness.

INSIGHTS FROM JAKE

I can't imagine living my life without being close to God. He is the reason I wake up every day with hope and confidence for what that day will bring. I know he has a plan for my life, and I know he will give me the strength to overcome any obstacles that come my way. I draw a lot of comfort from his Word, and it helps me when I feel frustrated or sad. It also gives me the will to think positively and have a good attitude. Knowing God is in control and that he loves me gives me great peace.

Psalm 29:11 states, "The LORD gives strength to his people; the LORD blesses his people with peace" (NIV). It's like knowing your parents are there and they love you and will take good care of you. It's the same with God: I don't worry, because he is there. God always has new things to show me. Every day I learn new lessons from being blind or just being a kid. I think I've developed an openness to God's ways and am willing to be used by his will. Staying close to God gives me peace, confidence, and happiness.

Follow Your Goal, Not Your Mood

In November 2010, 365 college students were asked to participate in a study to determine the effect of mood on decision making. The study was reported in the *Journal of Consumer Research*.

The students were divided into several different groups and shown different video clips that were intended to create either a positive or a negative mood. Then the students were asked to move to a different room to complete a questionnaire. While there, they were given a choice of a healthy or an unhealthy snack. Those who were shown the positive mood video selected the healthy snack significantly more often.

Next, the researchers changed the population of students to see if students with different levels of physical fitness would choose differently. But the result was always the same. Mood won out almost every time. The researchers concluded that mood can be influenced by outside factors, and that mood influences our ability to make choices.

Mood is powerful. Let's face it: sometimes we feel like it and sometimes we don't. We make a lot of decisions each day based on moods. If we stopped and thought about how many decisions were influenced by mood, we'd likely be surprised. How many times have you, at the moment of choice, thought to yourself, *I don't feel like it*? It happens all the time. We need to understand the role mood has in our decision making and our willingness to do the tough stuff in life.

Pursuing Our Dreams Makes Us Happier

Years ago, after I turned forty, I decided it was time to pursue my lifelong goal to earn a PhD. There were a lot of reasons not to do it. I already had a master's degree. I was busy with a full-time job. My wife and I had five children. There was no time to go back to school. I didn't need a PhD for my career; it was progressing well. But for some reason, this goal pressed upon my mind over and over again. I couldn't shake it.

So I decided to check it out. As I looked into the possibility, I learned the university had an exceptional PhD program with a professor whom I really admired. I sat down with the school and explained my situation and busy schedule. They were helpful. Together we worked out a plan; it would take a bit longer than other students to complete the degree, but I found a way without sacrificing my important family time.

As I threw myself into the classes, I learned something interesting. Classes and lessons didn't make me happy, but the experiences I had and the people I met brought amazing depth and richness to my life. The small things I learned about myself gave me better perspective about who I was and who I could become. What I learned made me a better manager, father, and person. Most of all, I learned how to learn, and that has made all the difference since.

Has there been a goal pressing on your mind for a while? For you, it may not be a PhD. It may be a goal to coach your kid's soccer team. You may decide to take flying lessons. You may finally get involved in your local church. Whatever it is, get determined. Get positive about something new. Get better at some part of life, and life will get better for you.

Change Your Language

Too many of us rely on someone else or something else to dictate our moods. We believe that happiness depends on what happens to us. We wait for our jobs to change, our marriages to improve, our careers to blossom, or our bank accounts to grow before we can have a happy disposition. The truth is that joy is not dependent on any of these things.

To lose the gloom, change your language. If you're gloomy, listen to yourself talk. You're likely backbiting, complaining, or talking poorly of others outside their presence. This type of language is habitually destructive. Once you start talking about why your boss is such a lousy person, you soon can see no good in him at all. When you can see something good in others and talk only of the good you see, it lightens your load. When you commit to speak only well of other people, you not only protect their reputations, but you also create a different disposition inside yourself. It's almost impossible to talk of the good in others and think of the bad in others.

To lose the gloom, change the phrases you use. Keith Harrell calls these phrases "bad attitude baggage" because we are always carrying them around needlessly. The phrases are "what if" and "if only." We use "what if" when we say to ourselves: "What if I lose my job?" or "What if I can't do it?" Asking ourselves "what if" in a negative way keeps the fog of gloom over our eyes. Sometimes it's frightening to think we may fail or make a mistake, but thinking about it is only a waste of time and worry.

"If only" statements aren't much better. These statements sound like, "If only I hadn't made that dumb decision," or "If only my mother would stop doing that." Making "if only" statements only serves to take away our joy. They lead us into the deceptive world of how things could have been different in the past or they should be different today.

Instead, try a phrase like "What would happen if . . ." That's a powerful phrase. Especially if you use it like this: "What would happen if I made this small improvement in my tone of voice when speaking to others?" Or, "What would happen if I smiled more often?" So invite positive phrases into your vocabulary, your thinking, and your life.

To lose the gloom, apologize. One of the most useful habits in life is to learn to apologize and apologize quickly. When we're in the mode of justifying an ill-advised action or ignoring a rift in a relationship, it's very hard to be happy. The more we justify our actions, the more gloom sets in.

When we don't apologize, it takes our focus away from the joy of life. Have you ever had a disagreement with another person and then bumped into that person again? Was it awkward? Did you think about it over and over again? When we don't sincerely apologize, we waste our time and thoughts on things that don't matter. It's as if we give our happiness away. We give away our freedom to choose to be happy. To get it back, apologize quickly and lose the gloom.

- Your life's course can change. You can raise your level of happiness by changing your habits.
- With a plan in your daily life, you can stop following your moods and start following your plan.
- By moving a little closer to God, a habit of happiness becomes possible in your life.
- Change you language, change your mood.

WHAT WE EXPECT,
WE FIND

Be not afraid of life. Believe that life is worth living,
and your belief will help you create the fact.[1]

—WILLIAM JAMES

n the 1993 film *Groundhog Day*, Phil Connors, played by actor Bill Murray, is a self-centered weatherman who gets stuck living the same day over and over again. The day he relives repeatedly is February 2, Groundhog Day. At first he's confused, but then, with no one else aware that he's reliving and repeating the same day, he begins to venture out and take unnecessary risks. He gorges on high-calorie foods, drives at high speed, and robs the local bank, knowing there are no consequences for his actions—he'll just wake up the next day and start all over again.

In one memorable scene, Connors kidnaps the groundhog, jumps into a truck, and leads the local police in a high-speed chase ending with the truck, Connors, and groundhog all flying over a cliff to a fiery death. Even this doesn't keep Connors from waking up on Groundhog Day again.

He repeatedly tries, with no success, to capture the affection of Rita, a television producer. Finding no happiness in his self-centered way of life, Connors finally explains his situation to Rita, who suggests he use his time to improve himself. So Connors takes her advice. He makes a change. He begins to take positive action. In his mind's eye, he sees himself in a new way. He starts helping others, rescuing town members from accidents, which he has foreseen, and improving his own talents. He learns to play the piano, speak French, and recite classic French poetry. During these never-ending days, he also gets to know Rita and falls in love with who she is rather than how she looks.

Day by day, little by little, Connors is transformed. He finds beauty in other people and the world around him. He learns what true happiness is and, as a result, Rita can't help but be attracted to him. When he gains her love, he is released from the curse and finally wakes up on February 3. He breaks the cycle, moves on, and enters into a new day.

Like Phil Connors, when we adopt a new image of who we are and who we can be, we, too, can break out of life's routine and learn how to be happy. Having a positive self-image unlocks our ability to act with purpose and live up to our potential.

The problem is that some people live with poor self-image. Life has beaten them down. They're in a rut. Other people have told them "you can't" or "you shouldn't" so many times that they believe it. They think that no matter how hard they try, they won't be capable. When they look in the mirror, they just see the same old person staring back.

It's time for a new image in the mirror. We need to see the people we can be. When we change the way we view ourselves, it opens up the future. We invite new possibilities. We start to fill our thinking with new thoughts and shove out the old thinking that has held us back. What we expect, we find.

What the Mind Expects, It Finds

When we take the time to see our lives as they can and should be, we take action. Visualization is the great enabler.

Gabriele Oettingen, Karoline Schnetter, and Hyeon-ju Pak studied the impact of positive image on goals and achievement, and published their findings in the *Journal of Personality and Social Psychology*. They learned that people are significantly more likely to achieve what they want to achieve if the following three things happen.

> **Visualization is the great enabler.**

First, you must have a mental image of the outcome of whatever goal you've set. You must visualize it. Think about it and see it over and over again in your mind's eye. The image must be positive and produce an emotional response. It must lift your hope and engage your passion. It must gnaw at you constantly so it drives your expectations.

Second, to bring your goal into reality, you must be able to simultaneously imagine the obstacles that might come along as you go about achieving your goal. You must visualize the obstacles and see yourself successfully dealing with them along the way. This is critical. A dream without reality is only a wish. To make your image of what you'd like to do become a reality, you need to think about and imagine what could get in your way.

Third, you can't get too discouraged. This happens to a lot of people. They have a goal. But when they think about all the reasons it will be difficult, they stop dreaming. You have to be able to confront the reality of difficulty without being consumed by it.

The research showed that when people only imagined what they could be without anticipating the obstacles, they didn't fully commit themselves to the goal. When people dwelled too long on the obstacles or difficulties, they didn't follow through. The unique combination of positive image and positive action led to the highest rate of achievement and success.

Ten-year-old Amiya Alexander knows about having a dream and the faith to confront reality in a positive way.

"It was 1:06 in the morning, and I was sleeping in my room, and I woke up in the middle of the night, and in my head I saw a pink bus," says Amiya. "I wrote my ideas down and I sketched out the bus and I colored it. I ran to my mom and I woke her up and I told her, and she was like, 'Can we just go back to bed? Tell me in the morning.' "

But Amiya had a dream of what she was meant to do. She wanted to start a dance studio for young girls who couldn't afford dance lessons, but not just any dance studio: a studio on a pink bus.

With her parents' help, Amiya has made her dream a reality. Now she helps girls, lots of girls, learn to dance. She has goals to open a Detroit-based performing arts center, study at Harvard Medical School, and become an obstetrician. Her positive image, sketched on a piece of paper with a crayon, is a perfect testament that what the mind expects it finds.

In her book *Mindset,* Dr. Carol Dweck says, "For twenty years, my research has shown that *the view you adopt for yourself* profoundly affects the way you lead your life."[2] So how do you get a positive view? Dweck argues it's through what she calls a "growth mindset." A growth mindset is a set belief that by your efforts, despite challenges, you can grow and become better than you are today.

In her research, Dweck tested the brain waves of people with and without a growth mindset. As part of her research, Dweck gave a written exam to a group of students. Those without a growth mindset were only interested in whether their answers were right or wrong. They had no elevated brain activity associated with what they could learn in the process. Even when they got an answer wrong, they had no interest in learning what answer was right. Those with a growth mindset, however, were interested in learning more than their test scores. When an answer was explained to them, their brain activity went up. Dweck demonstrated that our mindset dictates our way of taking action.

You are no different. If you have a growth mindset, you're more engaged, more interested. Dweck's research shows that with a growth mindset, you don't have to be perfect today to stay energized toward a goal. You have faith that you can learn and make progress. Does that mean a positive view will magically make good things happen? No. It means a positive view will turn your image to action. When it does, good things happen.

INSIGHTS FROM JAKE

When I think of what my potential is and what I'll be doing ten years from now, I hope to become the first blind golfer competing in the PGA. I see myself winning tournaments and using my gifts to help motivate and inspire others to strive for their goals. I want to bring glory to God and demonstrate that circumstances don't have to stop someone from following his dream. I picture myself educating, motivating, and helping other people.

In ten years, I will be a University of Southern California graduate and I hope to continue motivational speaking. I hope to bring passion, peace, and possibility to the world around me.

I don't know where I got my positive image of my future. Many people have encouraged me in my life. My parents, grandparents, and

> Most important, reading God's Word and knowing that he is going to be there for me gives me the freedom to have a positive outlook for my future.

aunts and uncles have always supported me and told me I can do anything I set my mind to. Nancy Mansfield, my mentor and advocate at the hospital, would continually tell me how smart I was and how I was going to do something great in my future. My teachers have taught me to work hard and keep trying until I figure out solutions to different challenges. My friends support me and help me.

Most important, reading God's Word and knowing that he is going to be there for me gives me the freedom to have a positive outlook for my future. I trust that he has a plan for me and that it's a great plan. Many people tell me that God has a purpose for me and that I impact other people's lives. My purpose is to use my talents to give God glory and to help others.

The Power of Positive Anticipation

Have you ever had something in mind that you looked forward to, like a vacation or reuniting with a longtime friend? How did that positive anticipation make you feel? Researchers have confirmed what most people already know: it's easy to act when you are positively anticipating an action or event. For example, many people will work extra hours with enthusiasm as they prepare for a weekend camping trip. A runner, anticipating a marathon, will run daily for weeks and months, all the while imagining the feeling of crossing the finish line.

On the other hand, have you ever had nothing to look forward to? Have you ever felt as if your life was in a rut, as if you were doing the same routine over and over again thoughtlessly? When that happens, it's tough to cheer up or wake up. Those feelings of stagnation result, in part, from what's going on in your mind's eye.

How do our imaginations influence our behaviors? The establishment of neural pathways in our brains enables us to repeat activities with greater ease. Your mind could be compared to a wheat field. The first time you walk across the field, you step on the wheat, smashing it down wherever you've walked. After one passing, the wheat soon stands straight again, leaving no evidence of where you have walked. If you walk the same path a second and third time, however, the path becomes more worn, and soon a permanent path is created.

No matter who you are, you likely repeat certain actions without thinking. That's because our brains, which are made to constantly gather information and develop greater capability, have cleared pathways for those actions. Anytime a connection in the brain is used, it grows in capability.

In the 1990s, neuroscientists at the University of Parma discovered mirror neurons. Mirror neurons are similar to the other neurons found in the interior frontal cortex of our brains. Neurons in this area of our brains fire when we perform any action. What scientists learned, however, is that mirror neurons in the same part of the brain fire when we see someone else performing the same action, particularly if we are paying close attention. Seeing the image of picking up an object creates similar mirror pathways as actually picking up an object.

The theory is that if we have an anticipatory thought or image in the mind's eye, the neurons in the brain fire, creating a pathway. Then when we do what we have imagined, we do it with more ease and success, almost as if we've done it before. It's easier because of anticipatory pathways. In this way positive images serve as catalysts to positive action.

Negative imagery works the same way. For example, have you ever thought about an upcoming encounter with a person with whom you've had an argument? You want to do everything you can to avoid it. Your brain makes anticipatory connections associated with the person, avoidance, and stress. So when you actually meet the person, you want to run away. Your stress level rises. You want to escape.

Dr. David Cooperrider says, "Much like a movie projection on a screen, human systems are forever projecting ahead of themselves a horizon of expectation that brings the future powerfully into the present as a causal agent."[3] In other words, what we anticipate impacts how we behave today and how we will react tomorrow.

Cooperrider developed a heliotropic hypothesis. He says that when presented with the option, we will move rapidly and effectively in the direction of positive images that are the brightest and boldest and the most illuminating and promising. In other words, we respond to the most positive images that our minds imagine. To the degree the image is positive and creates strong feelings that capture our attention, the more rapidly we respond.

Live Without Limits

Without any reason to think we can't, we sometimes do the impossible. George Bernard Dantzig was an American mathematical scientist who brought about significant discoveries in the areas of computer science and statistics. He is best known for his development of the simplex algorithm. In computing science, the algorithm can determine whether a solution exists for a complex linear problem. Dantzig was the professor emeritus of transportation sciences and professor of computer science at Stanford University.

What made Dantzig most famous, however, is a story from his days as a student. In 1939, while he was a graduate student at UC Berkeley, he was late for a class. His professor, the statistician Jerzy Neyman, had written two examples of famously unsolved statistics problems on the blackboard.

When Dantzig arrived, he assumed that the two problems on the board were the homework assignment for the day. He wrote them down and went home to work on them.

According to Dantzig, as he worked on the problems, they "seemed

WHAT WE EXPECT, WE FIND

to be a little harder than usual."[4] Despite the difficulty, Dantzig solved the problems and handed them in to his professor, even though he thought they were likely overdue at the time. The professor, amazed at Dantzig's brilliance, prepared Dantzig's responses for publication.

How did Dantzig solve problems that up until that point had been impossible to solve? Was it because, unlike the rest of the class, he wasn't told that the problems were impossible? More than likely, it was because he had the talent *and* because he assumed they could be solved.

Unlike, Dantzig when we face a challenge or possibility, we buy into the negative presumption that we can't do it. We listen to the negative language around us. It keeps us from attempting what might otherwise be within our power to do.

In 1952, long-distance swimming champion Florence Chadwick attempted to swim from Catalina Island to the California coast, a distance of twenty-six miles. The ocean was ice-cold. The fog was thick. As was typical with all her long-distance swims, she was flanked by small boats that moved alongside her to watch for sharks. They were also there to help if she got hurt, experienced cramping, or grew tired. After she had been in the water for fifteen hours and fifty-five minutes, Florence began to doubt her ability and she told her mother, who was in one of the boats, that she didn't think she could make it. She couldn't see in front of her and couldn't see the distance to the coastline. With only one-half mile to go, Florence pulled out of the water. When the fog cleared, she realized she was only a short distance from shore.

Two months later, Chadwick attempted the swim again. The thick fog set in just as it had before. This time, however, she was undeterred. She kept the image of the coastline in her mind. After thirteen hours, forty-seven minutes, and fifty-five seconds, she reached the California shore, breaking a twenty-seven-year-old record by more than two hours and becoming the first woman to complete the swim.

Both Dantzig and Chadwick teach us an important lesson: to

believe we can, we have to lose the images that hold us back and see (either with our eyes or our mind's eye) the possible outcome before us.

INSIGHTS FROM EMMA

My parents have been very encouraging to me. They encourage me in everything I try and they encourage me to be good at anything I do. Also, they encourage me to believe in myself and pursue my dreams. What I've learned is that in life you have to go for it! The sky is the limit.

> "You only have one shot at life, so you have to pursue your goals, live life to the fullest, and have fun doing what you love."
>
> —EMMA

I've learned so much from my brother, Jake. He taught me you can't let bumps in the road, even if they're big bumps, keep you from doing what you want to do. You should live life to the fullest, and I think Jake is the perfect example of that. Nothing can stop him from fulfilling his goal of going to the PGA except himself. I am certain that one day, I'll be watching PGA golf on television and see Jake there with all the other professional golfers.

I believe nothing can stop you from fulfilling your dreams except you. You only have one shot at life, so you have to pursue your goals, live life to the fullest, and have fun doing what you love.

In June 2010, the *New York Times* reported on a study done by two professors from the University of Pennsylvania. These professors used laser technology to measure the distance and success rates of more than 1.6 million golf putts of professional golfers on the PGA tour. What they learned is that when golfers on the PGA tour are facing a six-to-twelve foot putt for par, they statistically make it more often than when they are facing the exact same putt for birdie. Why? In economic terms, it's called "loss aversion." For whatever reason, the golfers feel a psychological need to avoid bogies more than to make birdies.

To the rational mind, this makes little sense given that every shot is worth the same score regardless of whether the shot is for a birdie or for par. But in the player's mind, he should step up more often to avoid having a score below par. This is understandable. In life we tend to work to avoid loss more than we work to gain. However, golfers who have the same success rate on birdie putts as well as par putts, can win more often and, according to the article, give the top twenty golfers about $1.2 million more in prize money each year.

It's the same off the golf course as on. When we let the birdie opportunities in life go by, we miss out on the best life has to offer us. Take a risk. Act on your dream. Life is so much more fulfilling when we put something on the line. As Jim Rohn put it, "You have to risk going too far to find out just how far you can really go." When we shoot to win, we shoot deliberately.

Believe in Others, Believe in Miracles

Our society seems to operate under the assumption that we need to eliminate mistakes in order to succeed. But this mind-set keeps us from trying anything new that might be risky. Why? Because there's a risk of making a mistake. We dwell so much on the possible mistakes that we don't attempt new things. This is stinking thinking. It limits the positive imagination.

In 1984, Daniel Kirschenbaum and three associates at the University of Wisconsin–Madison tested this concept among inexperienced bowlers.

Half of the bowlers bowled a game and then were replayed images of what they did wrong. The other half were shown repeated images of what they did well. In a subsequent game, the group that was shown the replays of the positive things they did increased their average score by eleven pins more than those who were shown negative images.

When we affirm others, we give them a sense of the positive in life. People need to be appreciated. We give life to others when we affirm them, build up their self-worth, and honor the possibilities within them. Too often our vision can become overly focused on our repetitive failures. We amplify common mistakes. A focus on problems doesn't solve problems as much as a focus on solutions.

At the end of the twentieth century, most surveys declared the Miracle on Ice by the 1980 US Olympic hockey team as the most notable sports achievement of the previous hundred years. Only thirteen days before the rematch at the Olympics, the underdog US team, which consisted of college players, had been crushed 10-3 by the dominant Soviet team, consisting of professionals. But coach Herb Brooks had prepared his team for that one moment—playing the Soviet Union in the Olympic games. Before the semifinal game against the Soviets, Brooks read his players a statement he'd written out on a piece of paper: "You were born to be a player. You were meant to be here. This moment is yours." The team saw themselves in a different way through their coach's eyes. His

> "There are two ways to live your life. One is as though nothing is a miracle. The other is as though everything is a miracle."
>
> —ALBERT EINSTEIN

plan was to outskate the Soviets, who hadn't lost an Olympic game in almost twenty years.

No one will forget the famous words of sportscaster Al Michaels at the end of the game: "Eleven seconds, you've got ten seconds, the countdown going on right now! Morrow, up to Silk. Five seconds left in the game. Do you believe in miracles? . . . *yes!*"

Miracles happen all around us. Albert Einstein said, "There are two ways to live your life. One is as though nothing is a miracle. The other is as though everything is a miracle." When we open our eyes of faith, we participate in some of God's greatest miracles, and often those miracles change us in ways we didn't anticipate.

Jake and his family learned this firsthand. While they were praying and hoping for a miracle to heal Jake's remaining eye, God gave Jake eyes to see what really matters.

INSIGHTS FROM BRIAN

When Jake was six years old, a cluster of tumors appeared on his remaining eye. The doctors took immediate action. Jake endured six rounds of chemotherapy, intense laser treatments, and surgeries. He endured the chemo like a champion. We fought the cancer with all the faith we could muster. In the end, when the doctors had exhausted every possible treatment available, the cancer still remained.

The doctors told us to "head down to the Braille Institute" and prepare Jake for a life without sight. We scheduled a return visit so the doctors could conduct another exam and plan surgery to take Jake's remaining eye. We listened but refused to go to the Braille Institute or tell Jake what the doctors had said. Something could still be done.

It was then that I saw God work a miracle in the heart and body of my little six-year-old son. That week at worship service, Jake decided to come forward during an altar call. He didn't tell us, but Jake was never afraid to demonstrate his faith. He leans on the Lord. As he knelt at the altar and prayed, I could see God working in the heart of my little boy. It was then that Jake decided to be baptized. He was baptized the following weekend.

A few days after his baptism, we returned to the doctor for the final exam before we would need to decide to remove Jake's eye to save his life. When the doctor examined Jake, he was shocked. The entire cancer mass and the lipid fluid around the tumor had completely disappeared. The doctor had no medical explanation for how the tumor and the fluid could have vanished since his visit three weeks before. He said it was possible for some shrinking or receding of the tumors, but he couldn't believe the entire mass was completely gone.

The doctors couldn't explain it, but I could. It was simple, miraculous, and wonderful. God had called my sick little boy forward and Jake had demonstrated his faith. While Jake would eventually lose his sight, God gave him a great gift. He gave him the gift of sight for the next six years. He gave six precious years for Jake to take in the views of life, family, and the world.

Some might say, "But God didn't heal Jake. Jake's cancer returned six more times. He didn't live happily ever after. He endured months of additional chemo and experimental treatments. He lost his sight. How could that be a miracle?"

I've learned that we do not see things as God does. Most often, the miracle God works in our lives is to heal our souls. Since Jake was six, I have often reflected on the story in Luke 5. In that gospel story, a man sick with a palsy is brought to Jesus. Jesus promptly declares the man's sins forgiven. When the Pharisees become indignant, Jesus asks them, which is more important, the healing of the affliction or the healing of the soul? He heals the sick man, who takes up his mat and walks home. The healing of the affliction is the outward manifestation and often temporary; the healing of the soul is inward and lasts for eternity.

Jake's cancer was temporarily removed by his faith. Jake took up his mat and walked with sight for a few years longer, but God had given him more than just his physical sight. God worked a lasting miracle in Jake, and he worked a miracle in me. God gave Jake lasting faith and reconciliation. God gave him the power to lead others to find faith in the same way.

Since that day, I have seen that miracle fulfilled in Jake's life. Doors have been opened. Opportunities have arisen. The miracle of healing in Jake's soul continues today, overflowing in its abundance. Jake, who has an overpowering desire to help others, is fulfilling his true mission in life.

I often think of what would have happened if God had answered our prayers and only healed Jake physically. That's what we were praying for—for Jake's cancer to be removed. If our prayers had been immediately answered, Jake might never have experienced the miracle of having his faith reconciled to God. He would have missed the rich and rewarding blessings that have come his way.

Nowadays, Jake speaks to a lot of audiences. No matter what the audience or venue, Jake is certain to deliver one clear message: "Brokenness, where it exists, is in the body, not the mind, heart, and soul. My mind, heart, and soul remain complete." Jake always shares his faith in God.

Since losing his sight, we still take the long drive on the traffic-laden Los Angeles freeways to the hospital. Jake still requires ongoing exams and procedures. But now Jake goes back to the hospital to support fund-raising activities, speak at engagements, and be part of promotional videos. That has happened because of the healing of his soul and the miracle God worked in Jake as a six-year-old boy. I thank God for

> "Brokenness, where it exists, is in the body, not the mind, heart, and soul. My mind, heart, and soul remain complete."
>
> —JAKE

the temporary healing of Jake's cancer and the lasting healing of his soul. God is indeed powerful.

A Winning Mind-Set

Jake has a mind-set that with God's help he will prevail, even if the odds are not in his favor. His winning mind-set is born in hard work. He expects to be an A student. He expects to be a PGA golfer. It doesn't matter that he's blind. He has a positive outlook on the future that he will reach his goals, and he is willing to work to make it happen.

When we work hard for something, it elevates our expectations of the future. In Carol Dweck's research, she discovered that people who didn't have a positive outlook of the future said they felt smart only when they didn't make mistakes or did something perfectly. Unfortunately, that's how many of us think. But the reality is that we all make mistakes. On the other hand, Dweck learned that those who had a positive outlook of the future said they felt smart "when it's really hard, and I try really hard, and I can do something I couldn't do before" or "when I work on something a long time and I start to figure it out."[5]

Ask any marathoner and he'll tell you that in a marathon, there is a certain point where you "hit the wall." It's when your body begins to hurt and you feel you no longer have the energy to go on. It's when your mind and everything else is screaming for you to stop. For the first-time marathoner, hitting the wall can completely rob him of his resolve to finish the 26.2-mile run.

But the second-time marathoner has something unique: the winner within. He knows that sometime during the marathon he will hit the same wall he's hit before, but he also knows he can continue running through the pain to finish the race. Armed with this knowledge, second-time marathoners can prepare themselves for hitting the wall and find the will to continue through to the finish.

Build Bridges

When you have a positive image of the future and confront the facts realistically, you learn and get better. You constantly get stronger and wiser from adversity. You can bear more challenges today because you've lived through them in the past.

As the story goes, a Christian missionary couple was called to Africa to serve deep in the heart of the continent. When they arrived at the coast, they were told they would be taking machinery to a missionary center at their outpost in Zaire. They had a whole truckload of heavy equipment. When they got the truck completely loaded, it weighed about eight tons.

That was a problem. The road that led to where they were going passed over many rivers and many streams, and over deep ravines. The bridges were crude, made of logs tied together with vines. Some of the bridges had 3T signs next to them, meaning the limit was three tons. Some read 6T. None of them read 8T. The truck was too heavy.

"What are we going to do about all that weight on those bridges?" the missionary's wife said. "We will have to leave some stuff behind."

The missionary replied, "There isn't anything I can do to lighten the load. We'll just have to reinforce the bridges." So that is what they did. They started out, and at each bridge they would stop and with considerable, sometimes dangerous, work (because the rivers were infested with crocodiles and poisonous snakes), they would cut down trees, strengthen the bridge, and rebuild it to the point it could carry the eight tons. And thus they delivered the supplies.

This is often how we look at life. In life, we often focus on the loads we're carrying and how we can lighten them, rather than considering the quality of the bridges required to carry the load. When we face a difficulty, we focus on the difficulty when we could focus on the bridge. We could, like this missionary couple, strengthen the bridge.

When we affirm the worth of others, encourage them, and build them up, we enable them to lift the heavy loads that life throws their way. The way to success is a determined course. It doesn't go around the weak bridges. It goes over them. Matthew 7:14 says, "Because strait is the gate, and narrow is the way, which leadeth unto life, and few there be that find it."

God's path requires bridge building. These bridges span the gaps in our character and the chasms of our weaknesses. Sometimes we look at the breadth and distance of the river we must cross, and we get discouraged. But God has promised us, as he promised Israel, "And I will bring the blind by a way that they knew not; I will lead them in paths that they have not known: I will make darkness light before them, and crooked things straight. These things will I do unto them, and not forsake them" (Isa. 42:16).

Bridge builders are engineers. Engineering bridges takes patience. Engineering takes faith. Bridging the gap between certainty and uncertainty, faith and knowledge, promise and obedience, or willingness and ability is not an easy task. But parents can be great engineers. They engineer changes in the lives of their children through positive affirmation.

I once heard about how engineers build large cable bridges. The cables are too large and heavy to string across the gap at first. So they begin by throwing a small rope across the gap. The rope is tied to a larger rope and pulled across. Then the large rope is tied to a small cable and then the small cable to a large cable and so forth. Once the large cables are drawn across the gap and secured, the bridge can be built relying on these large cables for support.

Life's success is built in a similar fashion. Let's say we see a gap in our character and decide to cross the gap. When we imagine our new character, it's as if we throw the rope across the gap. Then with some success from positive action, we throw a larger rope, and then a cable that will hold the bridge we use to cross over our past habits to a new way of life.

INSIGHTS FROM BRIAN AND CINDY

We've had to cross some pretty difficult rivers in life. Some have been easier than others, some life-changing. To cross those rivers, we've had to engineer and build a few bridges of our own. These bridges spanned life's cruel rivers and led to places that none of us could comprehend or truly fathom. We've had to face challenges we ostensibly knew nothing about. How could a parent possibly know how to build a bridge for a child who was losing his sight? To be honest, at times we didn't know how we were going to get to the other side.

The strength to build these bridges came from God. We couldn't do it on our own. Nor did we have to. God helped us construct a way to cross this obstacle in our life. He gave us the blueprint for this daunting bridge. It began as a blueprint of faith: faith in God's promises for hope and a future. Looking back now, this blueprint was enough. It was sufficient. That blueprint of faith became a bridge of faith. This bridge was absolutely scary and narrow, but it was solid. The architecture was perfect. The integrity and quality of the design was beyond reproach. Most important, all of us recognized that the bridge had been paid for. The bridge had been a gift from above.

As we crossed the bridge with Jake and courageously faced what we had to face, it wasn't joyful at the time, but today we have great joy. Although we had to face Jake's blindness in a matter of weeks, we already had a head start on our bridge. The foundation was already in place: we had a firm relationship with the architect, a strong personal relationship with God. We understood that relationship and knew the importance of remaining grateful in all circumstances. We had a foundation upon which to build.

Now that we've crossed the bridge and have seen our faith tested, we are more certain than ever of God's goodness. We're also grateful for what Jake and Emma have learned along the way. Jake will pass along the wisdom of faith to his children, and so will Emma. They will have bridges of faith to walk across during all life's challenges. We recognize the light of the Lord can shine on any pathway at any time if we will but stand ready.

Dump the Fear

Do you remember the first public speech you ever gave? How about the first time you played the piano or sang a song in public? Or the first time you played a sport in front of an audience? If you do, then you remember feeling the fear of failure. Fear of failure often keeps us from attempting to do the positive things we imagine for ourselves in life. No one wants to fail.

It's one thing to imagine what we can do, but it's an entirely different thing to overcome the fear of failure and take deliberate action. How can we dump the fear and move in the direction of our good intentions?

Develop a plan of action

When you have a plan of action, you can focus on the plan rather than on what could ultimately go wrong. A plan allows you to break the goal into simple steps that seem doable. Many of us take more time to plan a vacation than we do planning our lives. In your plan, set realistic time frames for important steps, and network with others who have done what you are planning to do. A plan can help prevent you from making costly mistakes and give you the road map you need.

Put the worst-case scenario in perspective

Stepping outside of your comfort zone can seem scary at first. It's often very helpful to consider the worst thing that could happen; you can then see that failure really wouldn't be that bad. For example, let's say you want to change jobs within your company. You are safe in your current position. By changing jobs, people might see that you aren't as good as others in that position. But what's the worst case? You will challenge yourself. You will learn a new skill. By learning, even failing, you will become a stronger and more talented employee. What if you enlist the help of a mentor in the new department who can guide and help you? What if you commit to spending a few extra hours in the beginning weeks and months so you can ensure your success? Then your risk is minimized. We gain strength when we envision the worst-case scenario and have a game plan to handle it.

Team up

The level of your commitment will see you through times of uncertainty. You can give up any excuse for failure by involving others you trust in your decision. Teaming up with others makes things seem possible.

Eschew excuses

Perhaps the most famous story about eliminating excuses is that of Cortés. He wanted to prevent a mutiny of his crew, so he decided to scuttle his ships. With all his ships scuttled except for one small ship with which to communicate with Spain, Cortés effectively stranded the expedition in Mexico and ended all thoughts of mutiny. When we scuttle our ships, we elevate our commitment, which can lead us to ultimate success.

Whatever the tactic, taking positive action will lead to the future you want for yourself. Imagine the person you want to become. Be the type of person who affirms the best in others. The benefits don't stop there. Through positive image and positive action, we learn, grow, become happier, and help those around us.

In Summary

- Positive images of our future help bring to pass great possibilities.
- To be drawn to a positive future, we must have positive images of that future.
- When you combine positive action with positive images, you create a synergistic combination that leads to success.
- Dump the fear of failure by developing a plan and staying committed.

10

A LEGACY FOR LIFE

You've got to think about big things while you're doing the small things so that all the small things go in the right direction.

—ALVIN TOFFLER

I f you're a child, you don't want to have grown up in Iraq during the last decade. For many Iraqi children, poverty is a way of life. Almost a million women have been widowed since 2003, and because unemployment is much higher for women than men, the children of widows suffer most. More than 23 percent of the population is living on less than $2.20 per day. The recent wars have caused a severe housing shortage, with more than five hundred thousand families left homeless and living in cramped quarters. The average number of people per room in the typical home is estimated at three or more.

Age five and under, mortality currently stands at 41 per 1,000, or 4.1 percent. Infant mortality is 8.5 percent. Before 1990, the country had sophisticated water and sanitation systems. Many of these were destroyed in the war. As a result of the water and resource shortages, Iraq can't grow enough food to meet the needs of its population and now imports more than 80 percent of its basic food, resulting in higher prices and crippling inflation.

Recent severe droughts have exacerbated the water shortages, as have the hydroelectric dams built on the Tigris and Euphrates rivers in Iran, Turkey, and Syria. The water shortage is causing the displacement of hundreds of thousands of people in both northern and southern Iraq. The country is heavily polluted. The UN estimates that only 17 percent of Iraqi sewage is being treated, and the rest is let out into waterways and rivers.

Children are often the hardest hit in the face of these circumstances. Many families are still displaced and unable to settle into homes and steady employment. Children go to primary and secondary school, but around 18 percent of Iraq's population above nine years of age is illiterate. School buildings and supporting facilities are in poor condition.

Despite all the tragedies that Iraqi children face, the most dreadful are the injuries inflicted from the war and its weapons. Car bombs, land mines, and other explosive devices rob children of their arms and legs and disfigure their faces. The injuries are devastating, especially for girls. Any type of injury to the face is a catastrophe for a young girl in Iraqi society. It most likely means no marriage and no children.

Thousands of Iraqi children have been victims of the war. Many have lost limbs, with no hope of a normal life thereafter. Who will help Iraq's children? National news recently highlighted one woman who is making a difference and leaving a legacy one child at a time. Her most recent legacy is a young man by the name of Wa'ad.

On what was just a typical day for Wa'ad in Iraq, school had ended and he was walking home with a friend. As boys do, they were kicking bottles as they walked. But when Wa'ad kicked one bottle it exploded. The bottle was a bomb. It tore apart his arm, leg, face, and right eye. Wa'ad would eventually lose his eye and the lower half of his right arm and leg. The explosion would leave the right side of his face horribly disfigured.

"I felt his life was destroyed," his mother told WNBC. But thanks to a US Army soldier and Elissa Montanti, his life has changed.

Montanti runs a tiny relief effort from her home in Staten Island, New York. From there she has helped 112 children get new prosthetic limbs, plastic surgery, and whatever was needed to give them back what was taken from them in the war.

CBS News reports, "She simply begs and borrows from doctors and hospitals, whatever it takes. She has traveled to the Middle East, arranging passports, cutting red tape, and getting wounded children out one at a time. Word spread among soldiers in Iraq that an American charity called Global Medical Relief is a lifeline."[1]

When Montanti heard of Wa'ad's story, she arranged to bring him to New York for four months of medical treatment that included plastic surgery on his face, artificial limbs to replace his lost arm and leg, and a prosthetic eye.

"How can we not help him?" Montanti said in an interview with *Newsday.* "He is a picture of this war."[2]

Thanks to Montanti and the medical treatments received in the United States, Wa'ad is not only walking again; he is also running and climbing up and down stairs. After living in Montanti's home for months during his repeated surgeries and recovery, Wa'ad and his mother went home to Iraq. At home he's playing soccer and living like a young boy should. He'll need to come back to the United States every year until he's twenty-one for more treatments and new prostheses. But he's now on the road to a better life.

Imagine if everyone left a legacy like Elissa Montanti's. Elissa dedicates her life and opens up her home to children from all over the world. One by one she makes a difference. She is leaving a legacy by the way she lives her life.

Why do some people leave a legacy while others don't?

Legacies aren't just wishful thinking. They're the result of determined doing. Your legacy is the life you lead. When you reach your final days on this earth, your legacy will be what those around you have as a result of your life. John Maxwell said, "What you do with the future means the difference between leaving a track record and leaving a legacy."[3]

If your legacy isn't on your mind, it's likely not getting done. If we're to leave this world having done what we set out to do, having made a difference, having met our true potential, and having become the people we want to become, we must be about our mission and the legacy we wish to leave.

But for many of us, we've never gotten started in earnest. And now, we think we're too old to begin. We think the best years of our lives have already passed us by. We think, *It's too late in life for me, so why change now?* But the truth is, we've never been more prepared, and leaving a legacy can happen at any age.

A reporter was recently interviewing a 104-year-old woman on her birthday and asked, "What do you think is the best thing about being 104?" The old woman replied, "No peer pressure."

Nothing, including age, should discourage us from living our legacy!

INSIGHTS FROM CINDY

If I could leave any legacy for my children, it would be that they know I lived a life in which I let the gospel of God shine forth. We all face trials. How we handle our trials leaves a lasting impact on our children and grandchildren. When a trial comes into my life, I know I have a choice to make. I can choose to praise God and rely on him, or I can complain, get angry, and become a victim.

James 1:2–3 says, "My brethren, count it all joy when ye fall into divers temptations; knowing this, that the trying of your faith worketh patience." I want to set an example for my children. I want them to learn to "count it all joy." They can even count the trials and failures as joy. I hope they learn from me that when they face difficult times, they can consider the good work God is doing in their lives. If they learn to give God glory during their trials, others will follow their example and be encouraged to do the same; through their example, others will see how the power of God can truly transform a person's life.

As Jake's battle with cancer has unfolded, we see more clearly how God is using Jake and his story to encourage others. People are amazed at how much joy Jake has despite his trials. God has worked his joy in Emma's life as well. She has so much love for God and faith in him. She has wisdom beyond her years, and her friends seek her counsel because they know she loves the Lord.

> "When a trial comes into my life, I know I have a choice to make. I can choose to praise God and rely on him, or I can complain, get angry, and become a victim."
> —CINDY

Probably the most important thing we have done to instill faith in our children is to live in such a way that they see us go to God for everything. We pray, we worship, we support our church, and most of all we talk about who God is and his plan for our lives. We look for God's purpose in every circumstance. We talk about how amazing and good God is.

Bless the Generations That Follow

Life is a collection of decisions. We accumulate the consequences of those decisions, good and bad, throughout our lives. We mistakenly think those consequences end with us; they continue past our own lifetime. We may think most of our decisions are harmless, and many are, but some of the decisions we make today will affect our children and grandchildren.

Children learn by watching what their parents do, not necessarily by hearing what their parents say. To be honest, I don't remember much of what my parents said. If you asked me to repeat what my father said to me as a child, I couldn't remember much. But ask me what he did and I can tell you volumes.

I grew up in a home where we prayed as a family every day. My father was a faithful man. He honored God. I remember the peace I felt as we prayed together. I loved those times when my father was the voice during our prayer. He prayed with great faith. I also paid close attention when my older brothers prayed. Boy, I wanted to hear what they had to say! But you know, because my older brothers prayed, I prayed. I'm thankful for the day my father decided to make daily prayer a priority in our family. Because of him, I do the same today with my family.

Parents, by their daily choices, can bless the lives of generations to come. Parents are the most important people in their children's lives. All their behaviors—accepting or critical, uplifting or destructive, tender or harsh—have a powerful impact on their children's identities, self-esteem, and faith.

No greater service can be rendered to our children than for them to see the principles of truth and faith manifest in our lives. Every time we resist temptation, honor God, express love, smile, or elevate our thinking, we rear a happier generation.

I once heard that living life is like running a relay race. When we're done, we're going to hand the baton to our children. When they're done, they'll hand it to their children. Every lap we run with integrity and love is more likely to be run the same way by those who come after us.

Through their trials, Jake's parents have learned about leaving a legacy of faith and patience to the next generation. Having a child with cancer isn't easy on a marriage or on family relationships. In fact, some research indicates significantly higher divorce rates for parents of disabled children. But the Olsons decided to make their relationship and family a priority. They're passing on to the next generation a new way of thinking and living.

INSIGHTS FROM BRIAN AND CINDY

No matter what happens, husbands and wives need to make their relationship the priority of the family. It's the hub from which a successful family turns. Every marriage needs God, especially during a family crisis. Seeing Jake go through what he had to endure invoked a unique set of emotions—anger, pain, and worry. At times, it would have been easy to turn away from the Lord, but we learned that those were the times we needed to lean on him. We needed to add another layer to our relationship with him. By doing this, we learned on many occasions that we were not alone. His presence was there with us. We were bold with our prayers. We spent time as a family in prayer. And we were often touched by his grace.

Honor Your Marriage Relationship. In times of crisis, it's easy to withdraw and be depressed. It can take a big toll on your marriage if you let it. You have to make time to communicate and hear each other's feelings. Say you are sorry when you need to. Extend forgiveness to each other. Choose your spouse each day. Show appreciation for each other. Say "I love you" each day. The stronger the parents' relationship is, the happier and more secure the children will be.

Be Grateful for What You Have. By focusing on your blessings, on what you have, and not on what you don't have, you bring optimism and love into your home; obstacles don't get first place in your thinking. Perhaps the toughest words in the Bible to comprehend, let alone adhere to, are in

1 Thessalonians 5:18: "Give thanks in all circumstances" (NIV). It's not easy. But we can assure you it will make all the difference!

Make the Most of Each Day. A family crisis puts everyone under tremendous pressure. Don't let the unknown or what *might* happen stop you from enjoying each other and the special moments that *will* happen each day. Be grateful for one another. Some situations can escalate or perpetuate in nonsensical ways. You can be filled with so much worry it seems unbearable. It is in these moments that grace must take over. Be forgiving. It's easy to be rude, cold, or indifferent when you're under stress. At these moments, grace and gratitude become powerful tools. Pray for help. At the end of the day, it sometimes takes divine assistance to get things right.

Take the Helm

Carsickness is motion sickness. It happens because your inner ear says you are moving while you're looking at the inside of the car that is not moving. In his book *Ready for Anything*, David Allen reminds us that we rarely get carsick when we are driving. How come? Because when you're doing the driving, you clearly see the landscape's ups and downs as well as feel them.

> **When you take responsibility, you move.**

It's the same in life. When you take charge and give up a passive position, you are immune to the typical things that sidetrack you. Small things don't get in your way. You have more discipline and drive. And when you take the helm, when you're steering your ship and take over your life's navigational responsibilities, you're much more likely to take action. When you take responsibility, you move. It's that simple.

In my experience, people who don't know how to make things

happen for themselves don't know how to make things happen for others. And the key to making things happen is to learn to drive. Take the wheel and get engaged in the process. Step up. Lead out. Move forward.

Here's a simple example. Imagine you have a goal to lose ten pounds. It's been a goal for several years, but you've never really gotten around to doing it. But one day you decide to "drive," to lead out. You're sitting with a few friends who are complaining that they need to lose ten pounds as well. You step up and take the helm.

> The person who leads succeeds.

"Hey, I have a great idea," you say. "Let's exercise, track our eating, and lose this weight together. I'll set up a summary sheet we can e-mail to one another to help keep track of our progress. If we really want to do it, then let's make it happen."

By taking the helm have you increased your likelihood of success? You bet. The person who leads succeeds.

INSIGHTS FROM JAKE

I want to leave a legacy that can help all people, blind or sighted, realize that they can do whatever they want to do if they work hard and are true to themselves. It's not important that blindness has happened to me; it's what I do with it that really matters. Taking responsibility for what happens to you in your life gives you power and the ability to take action and make good choices. I have a goal to play golf in the PGA. Because I'm blind, I have to work harder and improvise to make my shots, but I also know that I can do it. Each time I practice or hit a great shot, it puts me a little closer to my goal.

I want to help other people reach for their goals and achieve them no matter what obstacles they are facing. I have a foundation called Out of

Sight Faith to support the fight against blindness and cancer and to help other blind children. I am active in several projects and continue to speak in front of schools, organizations, churches, and companies to share my faith and my experiences of overcoming adversity.

> "It's not important that blindness has happened to me; it's what I do with it that really matters."
>
> —JAKE

Recently I spoke in front of four thousand junior high and high school students at a youth rally and shared my faith and experiences. I'm sure there were many of those four thousand teenagers who were struggling with something in their lives, or needed the motivation to overcome some form of adversity. I tried to talk from the heart. I stood tall and spoke openly about my journey.

I pray I made a difference. If at the end of the evening the students talked about "Jake not being stopped in life" or said, "Jake was unwilling to let circumstances stop him," I will have served myself and them well. Our world could be a better place if we encouraged one another to take responsibility for our own lives, and helped one another find ways to overcome the obstacles in our paths.

Do the Right Thing with the Right Motive

I recently attended the funeral of a close friend. In attendance were hundreds of people he had influenced for the better. Three generations of his family were there. His children, grandchildren, and great-grandchildren loved and adored him. By his example, he left a legacy of love and integrity. He was a good, giving man. As I sat thinking of his life and legacy, my thoughts turned to my own life. I imagined what my funeral would be like. What would be said about me?

As I sat pondering, it occurred to me that I didn't want my funeral to happen anytime soon. I've spent too much time on things that don't matter. I haven't fully lived a life that defines who I want to be. As I thought about my funeral, it wasn't success at work or achievements in the world that mattered to me. I thought instead about how I could serve. I thought about what kind of man I am more than what kind of success I've attained.

W. Clement Stone said, "Have the courage to say no. Have the courage to face the truth. Do the right thing because it is right. These are the magic keys to living your life with integrity." There is great power in doing things for the right reason. In fact, when you choose a legacy based on doing the right thing, it gives your life clear direction.

Brian Davis isn't the best-known professional golfer on the PGA Tour. But on April 18, 2010, Davis finally arrived at the place he'd always dreamed of: in a play-off with Jim Furyk for the PGA championship at the Verizon Heritage Tournament. If he won, he'd take home $1 million in prize money and fulfill a lifetime goal of winning a PGA championship.

Davis's shot on the final hole went into the rough. He was hitting his pitch from the hazard near Calibogue Sound when he nicked a reed in his backswing. He barely nudged the reed, ever so slightly. To everyone watching, the nudge was imperceptible. But Davis was pretty sure he knew what had happened. Rule 13.4 in the *Rules of Golf* says that a loose impediment cannot be moved during the swing's takeaway in a hazard. The violation would result in a two-stroke penalty and almost certainly cost him the tournament.

Davis called over the rules official, Slugger White of the PGA Tour, to confirm what he suspected had happened. Davis was straightforward, he made the call; video replay would confirm what had happened.

He gained no advantage from flicking the reed and did not do so intentionally. It would have been easy to pretend it didn't happen or to justify why it didn't need to be called.

Have you ever watched a basketball game and observed a player claiming the basketball went out of bounds off the hand of the other player in an attempt to persuade the official to make the wrong call? It happens all the time in the NBA. Not in golf. Not for Davis. Davis walked away with $411,000 less than Furyk that day.

Tournaments will come and go, but Davis's story will be repeated over and over again as a result of his doing the right thing. In fact, his legacy may be his honesty more than his success in golf.

Doing the right thing usually means serious sacrifice. It often means choosing a more difficult course of action. That's why few people choose it. But we become our best and truest selves when we do.

We're led to believe that if only this or that circumstance were different in our lives, then we could get back to doing the right things. The truth is that there is never a convenient time to do the right thing. You can be successful in your career, earn a lot of money, have a large house, or earn significant honors, and still flunk life.

If you're not happy with who you are or what path you're traveling in life, if you don't feel that you've met your true potential, then maybe you need to live consistently with your moral compass. You need to do what you know is right, regardless of the circumstances or consequences. This will leave a legacy that will last for generations and give you a sense of personal fulfillment that changes who you are inside.

In the Golden Age of Tuscan sculpture, white Carrara marble (like that used for Michelangelo's *David*) was the preferred choice of sculptors commissioned by the wealthiest patrons. Sculpting in Carrara marble was neither fast nor easy. The artist had to chip the marble off very carefully, layer by layer. Any mistake could be disastrous. The marble could easily crack. Sculptors who were less talented would often scar the marble.

But rather than throw away the expensive block of stone, they would resort to subterfuge. They would apply soft white wax to hide the flaw. The flaw wouldn't likely be discovered until after the fee had been paid and collected. As this became more and more common, buyers became more discriminating and careful. They wouldn't accept a sculpture until it had been examined. At the time of examination, the highest standard of excellence was given the name *sine cere*, meaning *without wax*. Later, these two words were combined to form the word *sincere*.

A sincere life is a humble life. When we are humble, we accept flaws as they are. Humility is perhaps the greatest character and behavioral trait we can leave to those we love. Sincere humility is strength tempered by love. When you do the right thing for the right reason, you are humble enough to own up to your imperfections.

> Sincere humility is strength tempered by love.

Recently, NPR reported that Don McCabe, a professor at Rutgers University Business School, conducted a survey of fourteen thousand undergraduates during the past four years, in which about two-thirds of the students admitted to cheating on things like tests, homework, and assignments.[4] McCabe says that students say the demanding nature of college classes requires them to cheat in order to complete what is required of them. Unfortunately, there are no great stories written about students who forgo cheating on a test because it's the right thing to do. They may not get the best grade, but they leave their legacies nonetheless.

Kirk Hanson, executive director of the Markkula Center for Applied Ethics at Santa Clara University, thinks the biggest rationalization for cheating is a heavy workload. He believes that sort of thinking can set cheaters up for a lifetime of cutting corners.

"Unfortunately, if you adopt that kind of convenience rationalization when you're in college," Hanson says, "it will carry over as part of your character into later life."[5]

McCabe says another commonly heard justification for cheating is that it's done to level the playing field. "They see other students cheating and getting away with it and getting ahead in this great GPA race, which makes them feel like they're being unfairly left behind."

The truth is, whether you're taking a college exam or a real-life exam, integrity is indispensable. When you act with integrity, you leave a legacy for life. You draw a blueprint for your future as well as an example for others to do the same.

INSIGHTS FROM JAKE

Personal integrity is the material we are made of. It directs our actions whether someone sees them or not. For me, it's knowing that I will do the right thing because I want to look in the mirror and respect the person looking back at me. Integrity is keeping one's word. If you do what you say, then people can trust you, and you can trust yourself. We are all presented with difficult situations at times and with things that seem very hard to do. Integrity is doing your best without excuses.

For instance, since I have become blind there are a lot of things that are harder to do. Putting away my laundry, finding my shoes, and taking out the trash take me a lot longer compared to when I had sight. I could complain that I am blind and say, "I can't do it." But I know I can do it. Using my disability as an excuse not only hurts others but also myself. I could complain that finding my glass of milk or plate of food at the dinner table is hard, but I recognize there are children in the world with very little food to eat at night and no dinner table at all.

Making excuses to get out of hard work or to keep from helping others is disempowering. Since I have become blind I have learned that the unemployment rate for the blind is 70 percent. I want to help change the perception in the blind community and society that a blind person is unemployable. Blind people can do anything a sighted person can. It may take a different method and it may be harder, but it can be done. Knowing that you did something right out of your own heart without anyone telling you what to do is one of the best experiences you can have in life.

A Legacy of Generosity

It seems that it's easier to give to those who don't deserve their misfortune. We are generous to those who are victims of circumstances beyond their control. We give to the Red Cross following a devastating earthquake or go out of our way to help a family who has lost a loved one.

What about being kind to those who are not kind? That's more difficult. Jesus taught: "Love your enemies, bless them that curse you, do good to them that hate you, and pray for them which despitefully use you, and persecute you" (Matt. 5:44).

As I get older, I am more and more convinced that for all the trying we do to leave a legacy in the world, the best place to leave a legacy is in our own home. The family is the basis for our society and economy. It is also the place where legacies matter most.

Years ago, my mother shared the following story.

I am sure my Sunday school teacher was unaware of the impossibility of her request.

"Class," she said, "I want each of you to promise that sometime during this next week you will tell your father you love him."

It sounded like such a simple thing. But I knew I couldn't do it. *Perhaps if I had the kind of father some of the others had*, I said to myself, *I could say those words to him.*

But my dad was not that kind of dad. He appeared to me to be insensitive, and the communication gap between us was wide. We had not talked seriously together about anything for years. Besides, "I love you" was something that I didn't think was ever said in my family. I felt I could never do what my Sunday school teacher had just asked.

After class, I waited until the others had left, and then I approached my teacher and said, "What you've asked us to do is good. But I think I need to be excused from that assignment. You know how my dad is, and well, I just couldn't say something like that to him."

But the teacher wasn't convinced. She looked at me and said, "No matter what your dad is or does, he needs to hear those words from you, just as much as any other dad needs to hear them. I want you to promise me that you'll fulfill this assignment."

I agreed, and during the next few days I felt a great burden. I knew it would only be lifted when I fulfilled my commitment. One night, after the others had gone to bed, I nervously waited for the right moment to say those words. Dad was smoking a cigarette and stood up to put the ashes in the trash. With a trembling, nervous, almost inaudible voice I said, "Dad, I love you."

He had his back to me, and he didn't turn around or say anything or do anything. I was sure he hadn't heard me. And so, weakly, I repeated it. "Dad, I love you." And then, very slowly, he turned toward me. My insensitive, untouchable dad had tears streaming down his cheeks. He put his arms around me and held me close and kissed the top of my head. That was the first time in my sixteen years that I could remember us embracing.

Today I'm a mother with my own big family. "I love you" is a familiar phrase, used often in our home. And what of my beloved dad? He has passed on. But after that day, I saw him become a man of faith, working diligently at serving others with generosity.

When we decide we're going to be kind regardless of how we've been treated, when we decide to express love even when it hasn't been expressed, or when we determine to live generous lives, others will see our determination and they will follow our examples. This applies to parents and leaders. Those we lead will follow our examples of generosity.

Sometimes we don't act with generosity because it seems much of the world is "in it for themselves." If you took your cue from the world at large, you'd act with generosity only when it was convenient. But you can take your cue from God. You can, in your family or group of friends, create and share a different legacy: one of kindness and generosity to everyone.

INSIGHTS FROM JAKE

I have maintained an above 4.0 grade point average in high school. I plan to go to college. I receive no special help or treatment in school with grades or tests; I do everything required of every other student. I have been given the ability to excel in school. I have kept up my grades and course work throughout my grade school, middle school, and now high school.

Even when I missed weeks and months of classwork with chemo treatments and surgeries, I maintained my grades. I know God has had a hand in my education. It is miraculous that I have kept pace and am pulling a 4.4 grade point average. It is miraculous that I am in honors chemistry and honors algebra. It is not easy and I am not sure how it all comes together for me, but it does.

The legacy I want to leave at high school is that I was an inspiring young man. I want to set an example for the other kids that proves our circumstances don't have to define us or our future. I want to show them that with Christ they are stronger than any adversity. I also want to be there for people and help them in their struggles. God has allowed me to experience adversity, and I can share my experience with those who are struggling. I hope people will remember me for my humor, my good nature, and my will to fight on. I hope people remember me as the kid who would not let the trials of life hold him down.

The legacy I want to leave in life is that I took my adversity and used it for God's kingdom. I have not let my struggles alter my future or my personality. I want to be recognized after I leave this earth as Jake Olson, a man who defined his circumstances instead of letting his circumstances define him. I want to be a symbol for hope and strength, so that everyone on this earth can say, "If Jake can do it, so can I."

When someone tells me how much I inspire them or how much my testimony means to them, I remember why I fight every single day and push on through the daily struggles of blindness. God put me here for a reason, and that was to help others. If I do not do that, then I am wasting my potential and God's plan. To see that I have inspired someone inspires me to keep fighting and to never give up.

Stand for Something

Perhaps no other image in modern history symbolizes standing for something more than the June 1989 photo of an unknown Chinese man who stood in front of a column of Chinese Type 59 tanks the morning after the Chinese military forcibly removed protestors from Tiananmen Square. He stood in front of the column of tanks with two shopping bags in his hands. As the tanks turned to go around him, he moved himself directly into their path. He was determined to stand his ground despite the massive size of the tanks facing him. *Life* magazine featured the photo in its *100 Photographs That Changed the World* edition in 2003.

Standing for something doesn't mean you have to stand in front of an armored tank, but it does mean you stand up for what you believe in. You may not have a photograph taken of your moment of courage, but it's likely that if you've decided to take a stand, you have a view of what's important to you and what you value.

A Man for All Seasons is the story of Sir Thomas More. More was the chancellor of England who was asked by King Henry VIII to endorse the king's divorce of Catherine so he could marry his lover Anne Boleyn. More could not endorse it. So he gave up his high office, income, and great household to avoid having to make his refusal public. He tried to step out of the public's eye.

But Sir Thomas was too well-known to drop out of the public spotlight, and his silence was widely and rightly construed as disapproval. He was put in prison until he would swear under oath that he accepted the king's title and new marriage.

"When a man takes an oath," Sir Thomas explains to his daughter in Act 2, "he's holding his own self in his hands. Like water." He cups his hands. "And if he opens his fingers then he needn't hope to find himself again. Some men aren't capable of this, but I'd be loath to think your father one of them."[6]

More kept his oath because it was the right thing to do. No other reason. Learning to make and keep promises, to others and to ourselves, lays the foundation for a life of legacy. It also increases our capacity to do it again and our self-confidence. When you make an oath and keep it, you increase your integrity.

The opposite is also true. When you make commitments and don't keep them, your integrity is eroded. You break down your self-confidence. You can justify your actions by telling yourself that *everybody does it; people do worse things,* or you can offer an excuse as to why you couldn't keep your promise. Nothing, absolutely nothing, however, can take the place of doing the right thing after you've said you were going to do it. In a world where it seems we are constantly letting ourselves and others down, standing for something gives us the courage to stand up in other areas of our lives.

Standing for something is extremely healthy emotionally and

mentally. A core foundation on which to stand and strive consistently helps a person feel anchored. Children thrive in a home with anchored values, where the parents stand for something. Organizations thrive when leaders stand for something.

Acting on our values may not come naturally at first. In fact, according to research conducted by Dr. Michele Borba, unless parents teach their children values, it is not likely to happen anytime in their lifetime. Parents are the most influential source of a legacy of values. Borba goes on to show that teens do not teach moral values to one another; parents still have the inside track.[7] When faced with a moral dilemma, teens are more likely to refer to what their parents would do rather than what their friends would do.

INSIGHTS FROM JAKE

My fight with cancer has given me the opportunity to stand for something in my life. I am taking a stand to help prevent childhood blindness by educating parents in the detection of different eye diseases that can cause blindness and death.

I am currently working with the Vision Center at Children's Hospital–Los Angeles on the "Know the Glow" campaign. This campaign teaches parents how to check their children for the glow in the eye that could be a symptom of an eye disease that could be cured with early diagnosis. I envision a world where blindness does not exist anymore.

I can stand for something in how I try to live my life. I believe to be true to myself, I should take responsibility for my life, love and respect others, and never give up no matter what. I think I learned this from my parents, but I also learned from my teachers, mentors, and from reading the Bible.

I learned the importance of loving and respecting others from how I was loved and respected while being treated for cancer and now after I have become blind. I have also been given the opportunity to make choices for my future, which makes me responsible for the paths that I am taking. The freedom to choose empowers you to take responsibility. I know that I can choose to move forward or choose to fall backward.

Most important, the lessons I have learned from having cancer and being blind have taught me not to give up. Things don't always go as planned, but there is always a way to achieve your goal if you work hard and stay focused. Having faith in God and his plan gives me the confidence to never give up no matter what.

It seems that when we know where we're going in the long term, we smooth out the emotional ups and downs in the short term. They don't seem as important if we know where we're headed. Small bumps in the road seem like just that—small bumps in the road. We aren't set back by interruptions. We know our end destination. Living your legacy gives you the gift of knowing where you're headed.

We can take the lead in our family to live a more abundant life. But we need to go about doing that today. So get into motion. Take the helm. Get rid of the trash. Get moving. As you do, you'll live a more fulfilled and happy life.

In Summary

- You can leave a legacy. You need to go about leaving your legacy today.
- Get in motion. Take the helm. Get rid of obstacles. Have a bias for action.
- Do the right thing with the right motive.
- Be generous even to those who don't necessarily deserve it.
- Stand for something. The result will be a better family and a better you.

ACKNOWLEDGMENTS

I continue to be blessed with the people in my life and the contributions they have made to me, through the development of this book and during the course of my life. It has been a joy working with McKay on this book and a treasure to receive all the love and support from my parents, my twin sister, Emma, my grandparents and my extended family. A special thanks to USC, the Seahawks, Coach Carroll, Ben Malcolmson, the TravisMathew team, Dr. Linn Murphree at Children's Hospital Los Angeles, Pastor Bruce Templeton, all my teachers (especially Mr. Walter Funk and Ms. Jenny Miklos), my friends, and, of course, my guide dog—Quebec—for always being there for me.

—Jake Olson

This book would not have come about without the help of our amazing agent Margret McBride and the hard work of Faye Atchison. A heartfelt thanks to Pete Carroll, who continues to lead with heart in everything he does. Thanks to all those who made a contribution to the content, edits, and logistics of the book: Michael Sackley, Andrea McDowell, Craig Flynn, Brian and Cindy Olson, Emma Olson, Kristen Christensen, Kristen Parrish, and many others who made this book possible. Thank you to the amazing staff at Thomas Nelson. You really do inspire the world!

—McKay Christensen

NOTES

Foreword

1. Judy Tatelbaum, *You Don't Have to Suffer* (New York: Skyhorse, 2012).

Chapter 2: Uncommon Faith

1. Jack Nicklaus, *Golf My Way* (New York: Simon & Schuster, 1974, 2007), 79.
2. Art Berg, *Some Miracles Take Time* (Salt Lake City: Invictus Communications, 1990), 174.
3. Ibid., 176.
4. C. S. Lewis, *Mere Christianity* (New York: HarperOne, 2001), 92.
5. Ibid., 205.

Chapter 3: Open Your Eyes

1. Myrna M. Weissman, "Advances in Psychiatric Epidemiology: Rates and Risks for Major Depression," *American Journal of Public Health* 77, no. 4 (April 1987): 445–451.

Chapter 4: Lemons and Molehills

1. George E. Vaillant, *Aging Well: Surprising Guideposts to a Happier Life from the Landmark Harvard Study of Adult Development* (New York: Little, Brown, & Co., 2003), 206.
2. Ibid., 273.
3. Ibid., 277.
4. Henry Wadsworth Longfellow, "The Rainy Day," from *The Poetical Works of Henry Wadsworth Longfellow, Complete Edition* (London: George Routledge and Sons, 1868), 288.

Chapter 5: The Winner Within

1. David Remnick, *King of the World: Muhammad Ali and the Rise of an American Hero* (New York: Vintage, 1999), xii.
2. Ibid., 147.
3. Ibid., xiv.
4. Neil A. Fiore, *The Road Back to Health: Coping with the Emotional Aspects of Cancer* (n.p.: Neil Fiore: 1995).
5. Brian Tracy, *How the Best Leaders Lead* (New York: Amacom, 2010), 50.
6. Sheryl Gay Stolberg, "Obama Tells Graduates: No Excuses," *The Caucus* (blog), *New York Times*, June 7, 2010, http://thecaucus.blogs.nytimes.com/2010/06/07/obama-tells-graduates-no-excuses/.
7. Gormin Woodfin, "Testimony: Clay Dyer: 'God Doesn't Make Mistakes,'" CBN.com, accessed July 8, 2013, http://www.cbn.com/700club/features/amazing/Clay-Dyer-070910.aspx.

Chapter 6: Our True Potential

1. Robert Kegan, *The Evolving Self* (Cambridge: Harvard University Press, 1982), 31.
2. Henry Ward Beecher, in *The Westminster Monthly*, vols. 38–39 (Westminster College, 1908), 107.

Chapter 7: Lead from the Heart

1. Used by permission.
2. Jack and Jerry Schreur, "The Simple Magic of Affirmation," from *Better Families Column*.
3. Robert S. Feldman, James A. Forrest, and Benjamin R. Happ, "Self-Presentation and Verbal Deception: Do Self-Presenters Lie More?" *Journal of Basic and Applied Social Psychology* 24, no. 2 (2002): 163–70.
4. Andy Cowan, Larry David, Jerry Seinfeld, "The Opposite," *Seinfeld*, season 5, episode 21, directed by Tom Cherones, aired May 19, 1994.
5. Stephen R. Covey, *The 8th Habit Personal Workbook* (New York: Simon & Schuster, 2006), 73.
6. Steve Bisheff, *Always Compete: An Inside Look at Pete Carroll and the USC Football Juggernaut* (New York: St. Martin's Press, 2009), 27; Pete Carroll, Yogi Roth, and Kristoffer A. Garin, *Win Forever: Live, Work, and Play Like a Champion* (New York: Portfolio Trade, 2011).

Chapter 8: A Habit of Happiness

1. *James H. Fowler and Nicholas A. Christakis,* "Dynamic Spread of Happiness in a Large Social Network: Longitudinal Analysis over 20 Years in the Framingham Heart Study," *in British Medical Journal, September 2008.*
2. Ella Wheeler Wilcox, "The Winds of Fate," from *Poems of Optimism* (UK, 1919).

Chapter 9: What We Expect, We Find

1. William James, *"The Will to Believe" and Other Essays in Popular Philosophy* (London: Longmans Green, 1903), 62.
2. Carol Dweck, *Mindset: The New Psychology of Success* (New York: Ballantine Books, 2007), 6, emphasis in original.
3. David Cooperrider, "Positive Image, Positive Action: The Affirmative Basis of Organizing," *The Appreciative Inquiry Handbook*, Cooperrider, Whitney, Stavros, eds. (San Francisco: Berrett-Koehler Publishers, 2003), 372.
4. D. J. Albers and C. Reid, "An Interview with George B. Dantzig : The Father of Linear Programming," *The College Mathematics Journal*, vol. 17, no. 4 (1986), 293–314.
5. Dweck, *Mindset*, 24.

Chapter 10: A Legacy for Life

1. Tanya Simon and Catherine Herrick, "Global Medical Relief Fund: One Child at a Time," *CBS News*, March 25, 2011, http://www.cbsnews.com/8301-18560_162-20046854.html.
2. "A Second Chance for Child Victims of War," *Newsday*, July 30, 2011, http://www.newsday.com/a-second-chance-for-child-victims-of-war-1.3062514#1.
3. James M. Kouzes and Barry Z. Posner, *A Leader's Legacy* (Hoboken: John Wiley & Sons, 2008), 180.
4. "Cheating in College is Widespread—But Why?" *NPR News*, July 19, 2010, http://www.npr.org/templates/story/story.php?storyId=128624207.
5. Ibid.
6. Robert Bolt, *A Man for All Seasons* (New York: Vintage, 1990), 140.
7. Michele Borba, *Building Moral Intelligence: The Seven Essential Virtues That Teach Kids to Do the Right Thing* (San Francisco: Jossey-Bass, 2001).

ABOUT THE AUTHORS

As a teenager **Jake Olson** has overcome the loss of both his eyes to cancer. Yet Jake's loss of sight has only increased his drive and passion for life. "It's just a new stage of my life," says Jake, and "I may have lost my sight but not my vision for my life." Since then, Jake has inspired tens of thousands of people at sporting events, youth rallies, and business conventions. Jake's story is one of tears, struggles, and loss. But most of all Jake's story demonstrates his *victory* over blindness through his unwillingness to give up those things in life he loves, especially golf. Jake continues to develop his game without sight and is now playing on his high school golf team. Jake's Out of Sight Faith Foundation provides support and resources for blind children.

McKay Christensen, PhD, is the president of a billion-dollar global consumer products company and adjunct professor at the Marriott School of Management. As a highly sought-after trainer, McKay speaks to audiences around the globe about his groundbreaking research on how adults learn and find happiness. With more than two decades of executive and management experience, McKay's teaching and writing includes servant leadership, transformation as adults, and lasting change. McKay has a heartfelt passion for helping others reach their full potential. McKay and his wife, Jennifer, are the parents of five children and live in Highland, Utah.

To hear more from Jake and McKay, please visit their website at www.openyour eyes.org.